WELCOM

Art Class

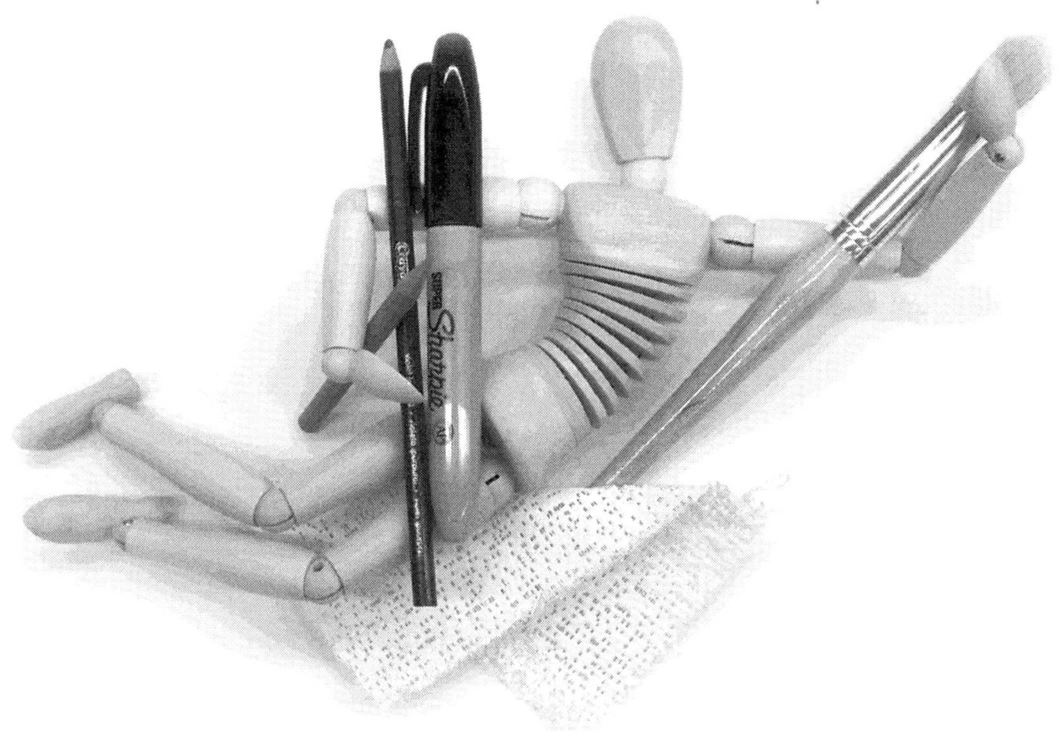

Your Name ______________________________ Period _____

Class: _________________________________

You will use this ALL year!

DO NOT LOSE IT

Teacher Edition

The Workbook For Art Teachers
A Classroom Companion for Painting, Drawing, and Sculpture

Fourth Edition, Soft Cover, Teacher Edition – 2024

ISBN: 1-940290-71-6
EAN-13: 978-1-940290-71-3

Printer: Amazon
Publisher: Firehouse Publishing

This book is dedicated to: Dr. Chris Craig of the College of NJ for showing me that teaching art could be more than I had ever imagined. To Ken Vieth who showed me what an art room could be. To my students who inspire me to continue being a teacher.

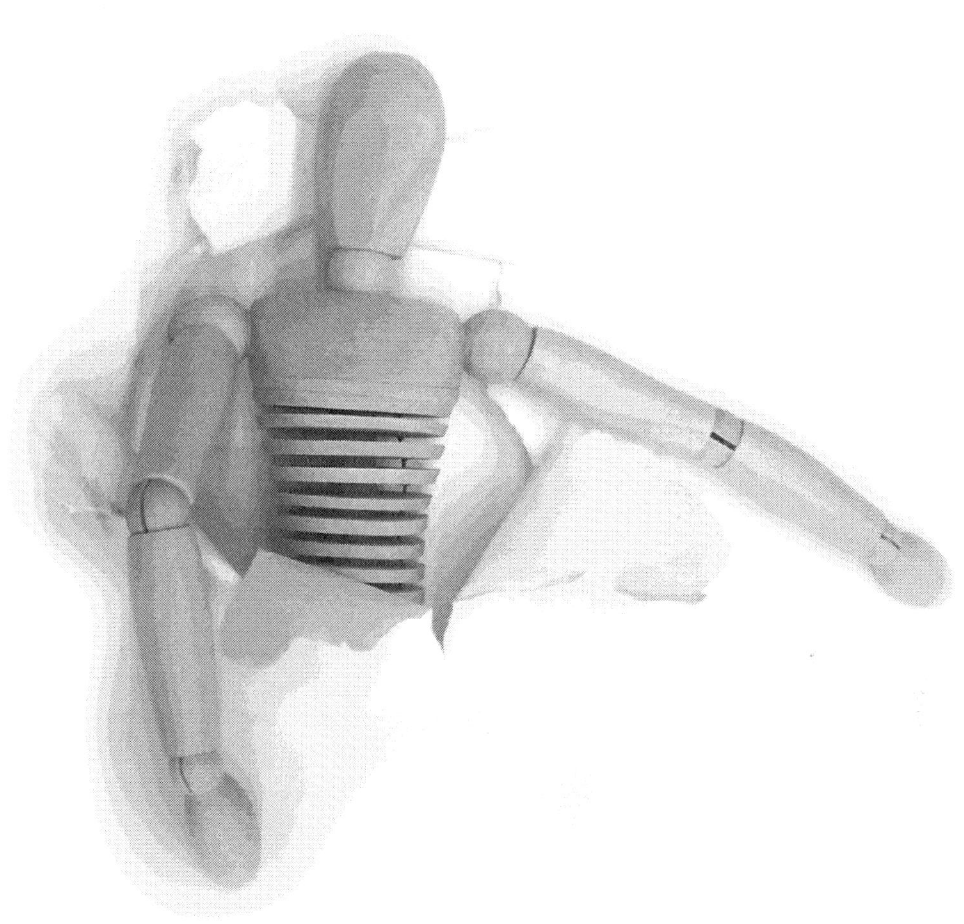

Student Achievement & Relevance

In a time when the economy is strained and schools must choose to make cuts, it is often the art department that is the first to suffer as it is considered peripheral "fluff" or a dumping-ground.

There is a wealth of evidence that a rigorous arts program benefits students. It may be the problem solving methods we use daily, or our natural "backwards design" approach that helps our students succeed. Art teachers know that these same concepts are what we already do, but they are only recently coming into the light as the new "cutting edge" of education. I think it is this and more.

Informal evidence from my school's guidance department indicates that students who take my course are 50% LESS likely to fail standardized testing. This is information that can grab the attention of your administration and Board of Education.

Art is the one class where the concepts of math, science, history, language, and writing can converge in a well-orchestrated, rigorous, and relevant program. We not only come to understand the concepts but we use them and manipulate them for deeper understanding on multiple sensory levels of thinking. I have divided this workbook by multicurricula units so that this concrete connection to academic core courses is more easily seen.

Does an art class lose its creative edge by incorporating other subjects? My thirty years of experience tells me that this integration enhances it. Students have a deeper understanding of the work, they come to see the relevance, and are more likely to "buy into" the concepts. When students ask, "Why do we have to know this stuff?" the answer becomes relevant through our daily approach, process, and end products.

ALL projects herein are designed to have successful divergent results, incorporate creative problem solving, and bring relevant connections to students' lives. This book is built for student success on many levels from gifted to challenged. This in turn is helpful in fulfilling mandated state and federal accommodations so that *no child is left behind.*

~ Eric Gibbons

Teacher Workbook Contents

Student Workbook Contents

Suggested Timeline of Instruction

1st Quarter: Art Elements and Color Vocabulary/Theory

2nd Quarter: Art Principles of Design

3rd Quarter: Art History Introduction

4th Quarter: More Art History, Research, and Careers in Art

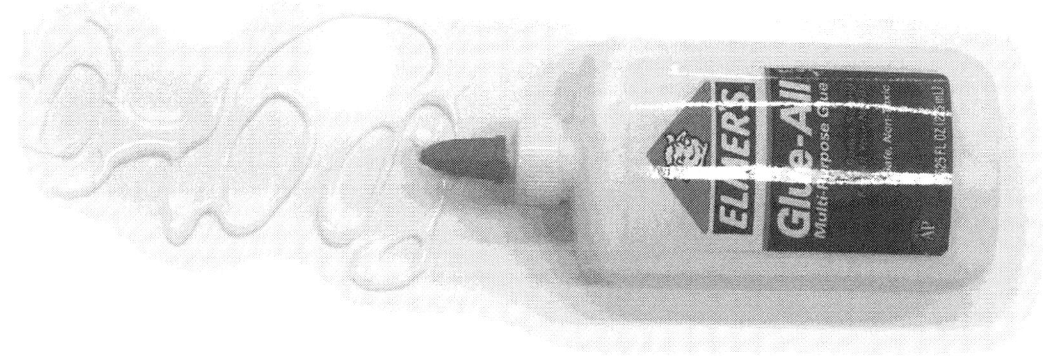

Teachers: I have a growing channel on youtube with many resources that pair well with this workbook. Please look there for updates resources.

https://www.youtube.com/egibbons

Student Workbooks <u>DO NOT</u> include all lessons or links in this book.

Welcome to Art Class

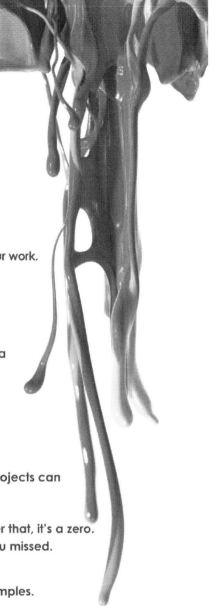

BE ON TIME...
- It shows respect and responsibility!

STAY IN ASSIGNED SEATS...
- So you can be counted.
- So you don't distract others or yourself from work.
- So you don't get blamed for a mess by someone else at your assigned seat.
- So I can learn your name.

RESPECT:
- For each other
- For the teacher
- For our materials

STAY ON TASK...
- Part of your grade is that you are actively engaged in your work.
- Hard workers do not fail.
- Chatting is fine, but the work must get done.
- Keep your volume low.

FOLLOW DIRECTIONS...
- For safety, good grades, and so that our materials last a long time.

CLEAN UP AFTER YOURSELF...
- I am not your mother, nor your maid, and neither are your classmates.

COMPLETE YOUR WORK...
- A big part of your grade is project work, incomplete projects can make you fail.
- If you need more time, ask to borrow materials.
- Projects must be in before the close of the grades. After that, it's a zero.
- If you have been absent YOU need to find out what you missed.

STAY CREATIVE:
- Be as original as you can, don't copy other work or samples.
- Do your own work, but its okay to ask for a little help.

____% of your grade is based on project work
____% is based on assessments like tests/exams
____% is based on assessments like quizzes or class work
____% is based on your active participation
____% Other ____________________________

Teachers Please Note

Most of the following worksheets are repeated in the back of the book with answers filled in. This is true in the student edition as well so that those with incomplete answers can have complete information for exams and tests.

This is helpful for students with special needs that you are required to provide additional study guides and information for. In this way their families may help them study.

Though the answers are in the back, I would not share that with the students until right before a test. Most do not explore their workbooks enough to know that many answers are located there.

Additionally, this workbook pairs well with the textbook, *The Visual Experience,* which I highly recommend. Be sure if you buy it you get a version with the co-author Ken Vieth, as it will also include many lesson ideas. However, if you cannot get access to these textbooks, all of the worksheets can be answered with standard dictionaries, encyclopedias, or the internet as a resource.

Please tell students to write their name on the inside cover, spine, and on all "pass-points" at the rear of their books with a color permanent marker.
This will help avoid loss or theft.

MANY additional free resources, updates, and assessments are regularly added to my blog at www.artedguru.com. You will find it helpful.

Art Class First Survey:

First and last name printed ______________________________ Period _____-______ Grade _____

Define Art: ____

____

How many years of art class have you had before this class? _____________

What do you feel your artistic ability is right now? 1 to 10 ________ (1 = NO ability at all, 10 = I'm pretty good at art.)

What do you hope we do in art before the end of the year? ______________________________

____

What would you like to get better at before the end of the year? ______________________________

____

Name some art elements (Line is one...) ______________________________

____

Name some art principles (Balance is one...) ______________________________

____

What is your favorite thing to draw, doodle, or make? ______________________________

Even if it's not art related, what's your favorite hobby or "non-school activity" ______________________________

____

What are 4 words you would use to describe yourself ________________________, ________________________,

________________________, ________________________, bonus word? ____________________

Sometimes schedules change at the beginning of the year, or you got a class you didn't expect and think you might want to change your schedule. Check off the statement you feel is true for you.

[__] I chose this class. [__] I did not choose this class so I might switch. [__] I will be switching out, 100%!

On the next page, draw the person sitting next to you. Their name is ________________________

Overview of 8 Art Elements

Elements: https://youtu.be/yN_M7pHwSSQ

A line is a ____________ moving through ____________. We can measure the ____________of a line and nothing else, therefore it is ____________ dimensional or ___ -D.

A ____________ that intersects itself will create a shape. A shape is ____________ dimensional. There are ____________basic shapes. The one with the fewest number of sides is the ____________. The one with the most sides is the ____________.

A ____________that moves in ____________can create a form. There are ___ basic forms. The one with the fewest amount of sides is the ____________, the one with the most sides is the ____________.

There are ___ basic colors. Basic colors are also called ____________ colors. When these basic colors mix they create ____________ colors of which there are ____. Color is ____________ light. Orange, red and yellow are considered ____________ colors, while blue, green, and purple are considered ____________ colors.

____________ refers to the weight of something; sometimes it is real and sometimes it is the way it looks. A ____________colored box will look heavier than a ____________colored one.

The roughness or smoothness of a surface refers to its ____________. It can sometimes be made by repeating an art ____________ many times.

All objects, art and non-art, take up ____________. Many art elements move through it. This art element comes in 2 types, they are ____________ meaning where the object IS, and ____________, meaning where the object is NOT.

The art element of ____________ helps us see all other art elements. We see everything because it is ____________ off of an object or surface and back to our eye. When it is NOT bounced back to us we see ____________.

Sometimes mass and light are combined and called ______________. This is helpful when describing flat images that look 3D.

PRINCIPLES OF DESIGN WORKSHEET

Principles: https://youtu.be/sbHPvnlT2Cw

Use a resource like "The Visual Experience" or the internet to define and explain this vocabulary.

Define CONTRAST:

Give one example of this principle not in the book, so I know you understand it:

Define UNITY:

Give one example of this principle not in the book, so I know you understand it:

Define BALANCE:

Give one example of this principle not in the book, so I know you understand it:

Define EMPHASIS:

Give one example of this principle not in the book, so I know you understand it:

Define VARIETY:

Give one example of this principle not in the book, so I know you understand it:

Define MOVEMENT:

Give one example of this principle not in the book, so I know you understand it:

Continued...

Define PATTERN:

Give one example of this principle not in the book, so I know you understand it:

What is a MOTIF?

What is the difference between CONTRAST and VARIETY?

Find any art image and list 3 art principles you can see in this artwork and how you know it to be true. Be specific so I know you understand it.

QUIZ

Art Elements

1. ______________ is the simplest art element and is needed to draw anything.

2. ______________ is the art element that is 2 dimensional. The basic ones are these three:

3. ______________

4. ______________

5. ______________

6. ______________ can sometimes be made by repeating an art element.

7. ______________ helps things look 3D in a drawing or a painting.

8. ______________ is reflected light. When we use a prism, we can see all of its components in white light.

9. ______________ is a shape in 3-D or a 3 dimensional art element.

10. Draw and shade ALL the basic 3 dimensional "shapes" below.

Art Principles

1. ______________ creates a sense of "sameness" to hold everything together visually.

2. ______________ keeps things from getting too boring by adding visual differences.

3. ______________ offers opposites to make the differences more obvious, even shocking sometimes.

4. ______________ gives a sense of motion, either real or by design.

5. ______________ makes a work feel settled, or complete on both the right and left in most cases. This principle is done in 2 ways, they are:

6. ________________________

7. ________________________

8. ______________ is a repeated design. It can be natural or mechanical.

9. ______________ makes one thing or area stand out more than the rest.

10. Illustrate & label one principle below.

Answers at the end of this book

Art Principles Worksheet *(Student Workbook has 4 pages like this)* (tiny sketch below)

The artwork sample is called:

____

by ____________________________.

It is from the _____________________
School of art. Please describe in FULL sentences
how you see the art principles used in his image.

Explain how the artist uses UNITY and where you see it used. Be Specific.

Explain how the artist uses CONTRAST and where you see it used. Be Specific.

Explain how the artist uses EMPHASIS and where you see it used. Be Specific.

Explain how the artist uses MOVEMENT and where you see it used. Be Specific.

Explain how the artist uses BALANCE and where you see it used. Be Specific.

Explain how the artist uses PATTERN and where you see it used. Be Specific.

Explain how the artist uses VARIETY and where you see it used. Be Specific.

Color Mixing

DIRECTIONS:

- **<u>Using only primary colors, fill in this color wheel.</u>**
- **Put a "P" next to PRIMARY colors**
- **"S" next to secondary colors**
- **"W" next to warm colors**
- **"C" next to cool colors.**
- **"T" next to tertiary colors**

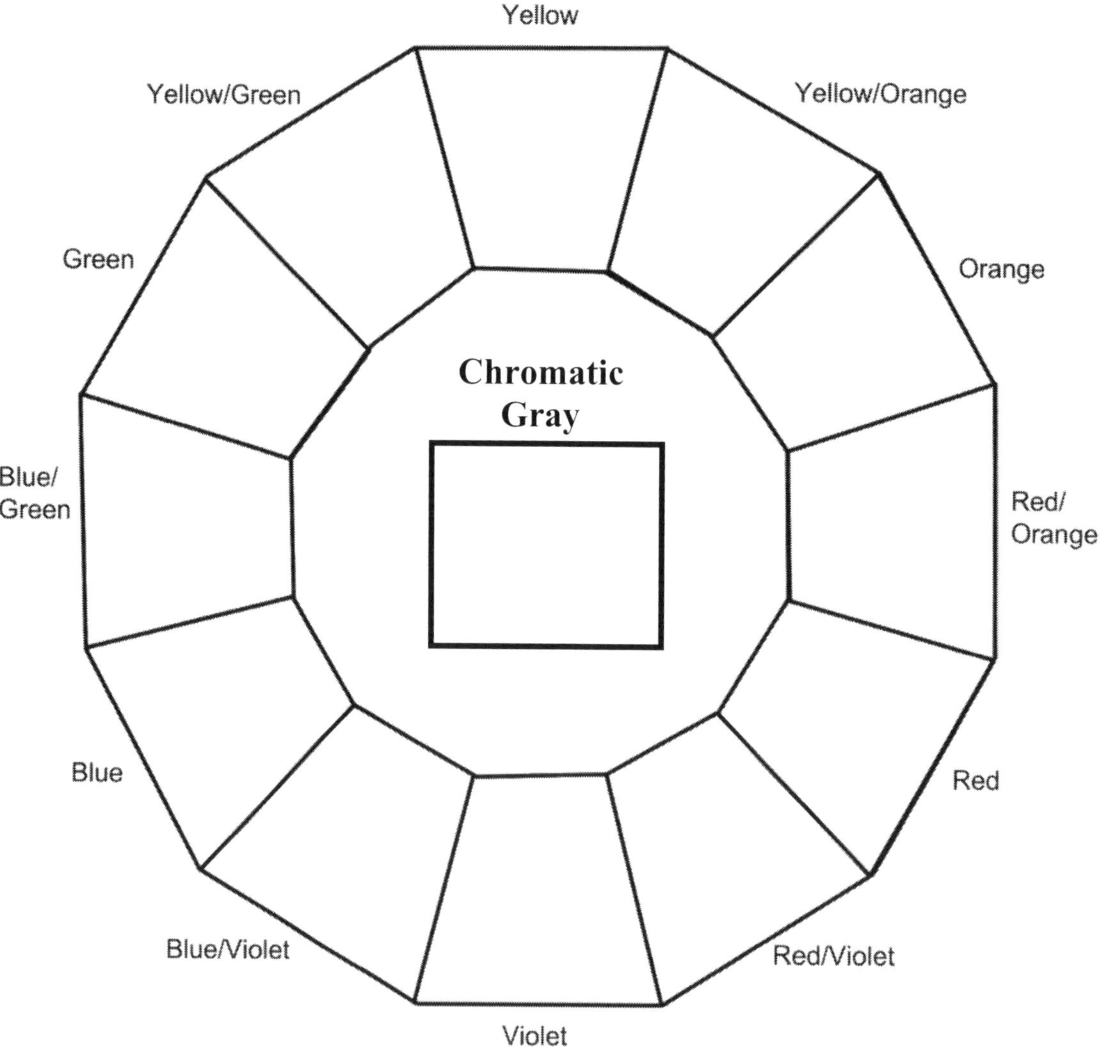

Tip: This can be done by layering primary colored pencils when coloring in. Use lightest colors first for best results... like yellow is lighter than blue.

Emotional Values of Shapes and Colors

See rear of book

Associations: ______________________________

Emotional: ______________________________

Associations: ______________________________

Emotional: ______________________________

Associations: ______________________________

Emotional: ______________________________

Red: Associations: ______________________________

Emotional: ______________________________

Orange: Associations: ______________________________

Emotional: ______________________________

Yellow: Associations: ______________________________

Emotional: ______________________________

Green: Associations: ______________________________

Emotional: ______________________________

Blue: Associations: ______________________________

Emotional: ______________________________

Purple: Associations: ______________________________

Emotional: ______________________________

Black: Associations: ______________________________

Emotional: ______________________________

Brown: Associations: ______________________________

Emotional: ______________________________

White: Associations: ______________________________

Emotional: ______________________________

VIDEO HELP AT: https://bit.ly/ShapesColors

Draw combination of shapes to represent yourself.

Using the color information on the previous page, color in that shape in a way that describes you.

FAMILY

Describe 8 to 10 people in your family including yourself. Include both strengths and weaknesses. ALWAYS begin with people living in your household, and then extend that list into family not living with you. You may include people you knew who have died. **If you do not want to list names, use a nickname or initial so YOU know who you are writing about.**

Create a mini sketch in the right margin below.

1. ______________ : __________________________
____

2. ______________ : __________________________
____

3. ______________ : __________________________
____

4. ______________ : __________________________
____

5. ______________ : __________________________
____

6. ______________ : __________________________
____

7. ______________ : __________________________
____

8. ______________ : __________________________
____

9. ______________ : __________________________
____

10. ______________ : __________________________
____

Family can be represented abstractly in either 2-D or 3-D

Video Support: https://bit.ly/FamilyShapes

The first sample is a watercolor painting where all family members are represented with shapes and color. Overlaps show the relationships between people. The second sample is a mobile of a family unit, where form and color represent each member of the family.

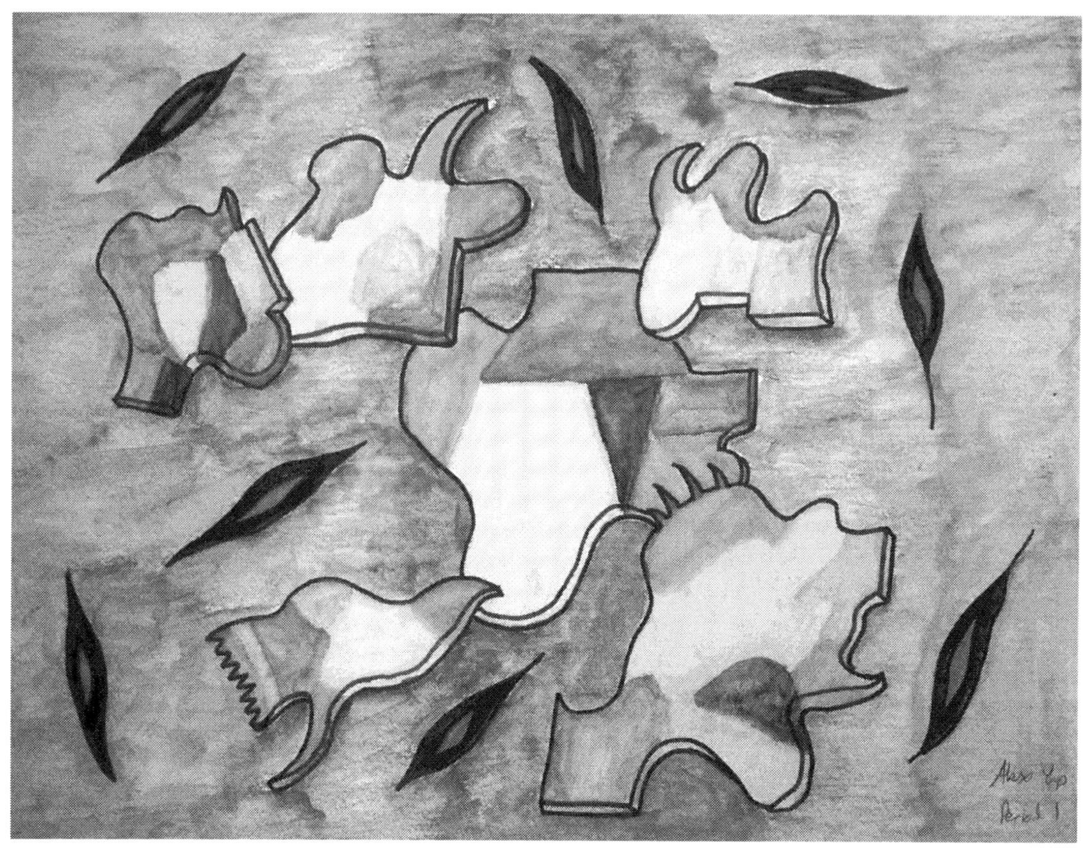

Video Support for Mobiles: https://bit.ly/CalderBalance

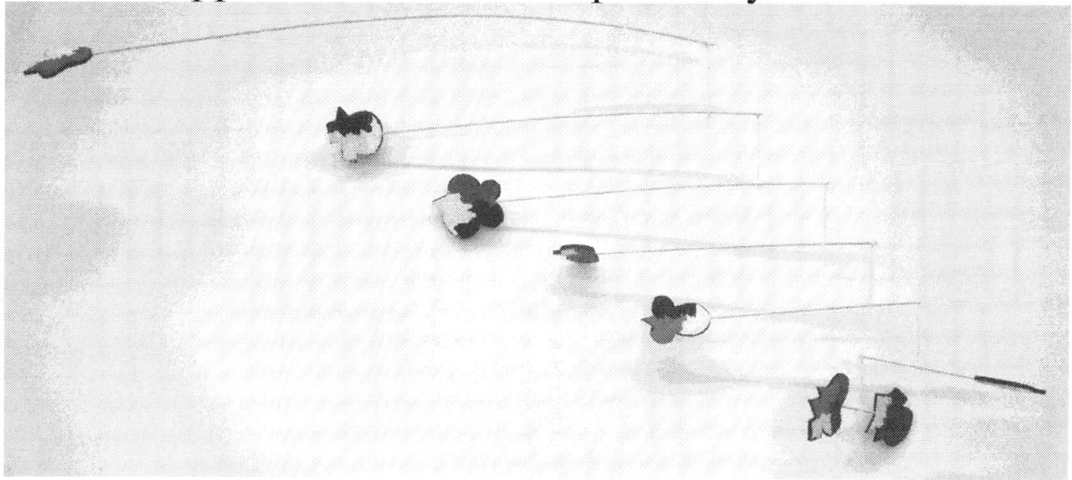

Color Vocabulary

These are common vocabulary terms in art. Which ones do you already know? For others, use a resource, like "The Visual Experience" or another like the internet to write a definition for each vocabulary term.

Value: ______________________________

Shading: ______________________________

Chiaroscuro: ______________________________

Spectrum: ______________________________

Hue: ______________________________

Primary Colors: ______________________________

Secondary Colors: ______________________________

Intermediate Colors: ______________________________

Complementary Colors: ______________________________

Triadic Colors: ______________________________

Monochromatic Colors: ______________________________

Intensity: ______________________________

Color Harmonies: ______________________________

Analogous Colors: ______________________________

Warm Colors / Cool Colors: ______________________________

COLOR WHEEL →

Use only the 3 primary colors to color in this diagram →

RED

(Violet) PURPLE

BLUE

GREEN

YELLOW

ORANGE

Guess what the mix will be first…
Then try it and write what it really made.

Red + Blue = ____________________ (________________)

Blue + Yellow = ____________________ (________________)

Yellow + Red = ____________________ (________________)

Red + Blue + Yellow = ____________________ (________________)

Orange + Blue = ____________________ (________________)

Purple + Yellow = ____________________ (________________)

Green + Blue = ____________________ (________________)

Black + Yellow = ____________________ (________________)

Black + Yellow + Red = ____________________ (________________)

White + little Red + little Yellow + VERY little Black = ____________ (____________)

Spectrum colors in order ____

Coloring Expectations

There is no reason to rush your work. We are more concerned with the process than what it looks like at the end. If the process is good then the product should be fine. When you rush things like coloring, it can damage the neatness and completeness portion of your grade. Though you may have been coloring for years, maybe since before you even came to school, there are a few things to keep in mind:

- You should use SMALL parallel strokes to color in
- The pressure you apply will determine the color intensity
- Try to stay within the boundaries you have set. (Stay in the lines)
- You should always color in layers. Nothing is the same color as a crayon
- Try shading with a neighboring or opposite color before choosing black
- Be patient, good work takes time

Though not every student is artistic, we expect all our students to strive to do their best. The back of this book has a color version of this expectation chart.

Video Tutorial: https://youtu.be/NGrEKizLSSQ Resource: https://youtu.be/4dbNPe1QcCU

COLOR BIAS

In a perfect world Yellow and Red make Orange… and they do, sometimes.

Why not always??? Color is not perfect. It is made from minerals and chemicals and nothing in nature or on this earth is 100% perfect yellow. Some yellows are a bit orange, like a bright sunny yellow, and some are a bit green like lemon yellow.

ALL colors "**LEAN**" a bit one way or another. This is called **Color Bias**. Some companies even label their paint so you can see which way the color "leans." When mixing colors, you need to choose colors that "lean" towards each other. If you do not, your colors will be less bright and even brown-ish. (This might be a good thing when painting natural elements like dirt, grass, bark, rocks etc…)

Color bias can work for you or against you, but you need to use it to your advantage.

AVOID BLACK in your paintings of nature. It is better to mix color opposites or compliments to make a dark tone. There is very little black in nature. Burnt wood/charcoal is black, some deep dark shadows may need black, but 90% of the time black should be avoided. It is often the easiest way a professional can spot amateur work. Black kills color and only in a few instances is this a good thing.

Mixing Watercolors: The lids of most watercolor sets are detachable for a reason… you can mix colors on the lid, but separate it to clean it. HOWEVER when painting a landscape, SOMETIMES it's better to mix right on the paper so the color is uneven. Nature is organic and does not have perfect colors. Imperfections in your paint mixtures might be a desirable effect.

Paint Brush Care

Paint brushes are an important tool in an artist's toolbox. They are expensive and need to be cared for properly. Some paints, like acrylics, can ruin brushes if they are not cleaned properly.

— Always use COLD water to clean a brush
— Hot water melts the glue that holds the brush together
— Be sure to wash the collar of the brush too
— Test your clean brush on paper before storing
— Store brushes with the brush-end-up

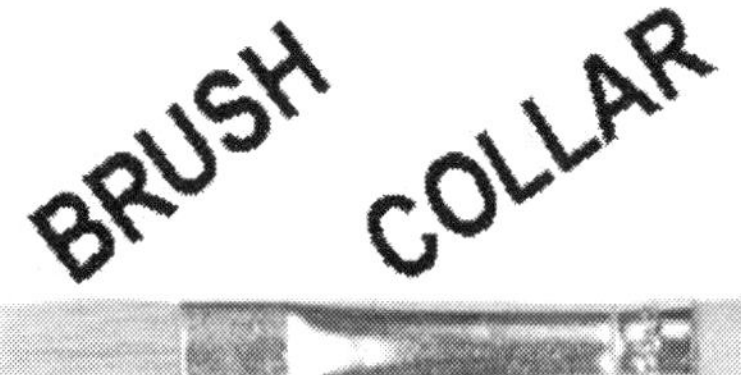

HANDLE

Teacher Video Resource: https://youtu.be/5MQr73EeHBA

PLASTER WORK

Plaster is activated by water. It is important to be aware of how you set up your area for plaster work.

1. Cover your table area with paper or plastic. Remove jewelry.

2. Keep plaster and water far enough away that the water won't accidently splash, drip, or spill on the plaster.

3. Be sure others near you won't interfere with your set-up or cause an accident as well. Several people can work from one bucket.

Once plaster has been dipped in water, it must be strained through the fingers and applied to your base or object to be covered. Plaster will need to be 2 or 3 layers thick to be strong.

If you accidently get water on a plaster strip, use it immediately.

Plaster cannot be re-used once it has hardened.

Smooth strips with your hands as you apply them. Without smoothing, one layer will not bond with the last.

NEVER put plaster down a sink. Not from your hands, not from the bucket. It will form stones in the pipes and be VERY expensive to repair.

— Wash hands in plaster water first
— Stir plaster in bucket with hands and dump in to grass or dumpster
— Let bucket dry and crack plaster into garbage

**Though plaster will come out of clothes, you may find wearing a smock is good protection. Tutorial: https://youtu.be/2_6pnuteHtE*

Liquid Plaster

Plaster is activated by water. It is important to be aware of how you set up your area for plaster work.

1. Cover your table area with paper or plastic. Remove jewelry.

2. Keep plaster and water far enough away that the water won't accidently splash, drip, or spill on the plaster.

3. Be sure others near you won't interfere with your set-up by accident as well. Several people can work from one bucket.

Determine how much liquid plaster you need (cup or bucket). Use LESS THAN HALF that amount of water.

Hot water hardens plaster faster than cold water; choose accordingly.

Add dry plaster with a cup or scoop or spoon by sprinkling a little at a time. Too much at once will ruin your plaster mixture. Be sure to sprinkle evenly all around your container so it fills evenly. DO NOT STIR THE MIXTURE!

Slowly add plaster until it forms islands in the water that do not go below the surface of the water. See picture above.

Once you have sufficient islands, you may stir. The more you stir the faster the plaster will harden. *(FYI: Plaster heats up as it dries; use caution if applying to body)*

NEVER put plaster down a sink. Not from your hands, not from the bucket. It will form stones in the pipes and be VERY expensive to repair.

— Wash hands in plaster water first

— Let bucket dry and crack plaster into the garbage. Toss cups.

Hint: *Acrylic paint or acrylic medium can be added to plaster. Acrylics make the plaster dry mush more slowly. Add 1/10 of acrylic medium to the water* ***before*** *adding plaster.*

Tutorial: https://youtu.be/RnG4X-bFUgs

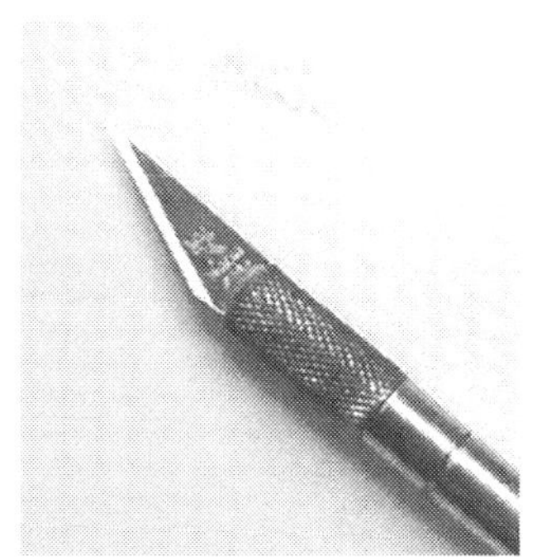

Razor Blades SAFETY

Tutorial: https://youtu.be/lgnfE0E2GrI

ALWAYS get permission to use any sharp tools.
— NEVER play with these tools.
— Taking one out of the classroom is ILLEGAL and considered a weapon in school.
— Check that the blade is secure and tight.
— Keep it capped when not in use.
— Protect table when cutting.
— ALWAYS cut away from fingers or body.
— Hold like a pencil for best control.

IF YOU GET A CUT…
— Hold cut tightly closed.
— Tell teacher immediately.
— Wash with running water.
— Pinch closed with paper towel.
— See teacher for band-aid or hall pass to the nurse.

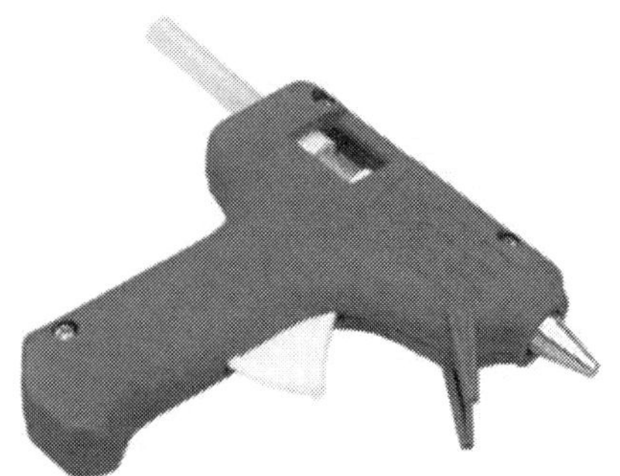

GLUE GUN SAFETY

GLUE GUNS can heat up to about 400 degrees. They will burn deeply.
NEVER touch the tip of a glue gun. EVEN the glue that comes out can burn badly. Use a craft-stick to move the glue if you need to. Glue guns stay hot for a while after being unplugged! A glue gun is NOT A TOY!

IF YOU GET BURNED, go to the sink quickly and rinse with cool water. If you get a blister, get a pass to the nurse.

Goals

What are some life goals you have? Things you hope to achieve in the future.

— By the time I graduate from high school, I hope to have :

— In 10 years I hope I have :

— In 20 or 30 years I hope I have :

— Before I die, I hope that I have :

List some things that can hold you back from reaching your goals:

1.

2.

3.

4.

5.

6.

The student edition has a sketch page next →

The student's sculpture shows his GOAL to be a great chef; the base is the thing that could hold him back. It is the money to go to a good college.

This page is not in the student edition

The Story of My Life

- First time to drive
- First hunting trip
- The time you won an award
- First time you caught your parents lying
- First time you went to a funeral
- Birth of a new family member
- First job, or interview, or first firing
- A time you were betrayed
- A time you got your first paycheck
- First trip outside the USA
- A time you had to move
- A time you saved someone's life or someone saved yours.
- First time you were tempted to do something wrong.

What are your 4 or 5 life changing or important events:

1____

2____

3____

4____

5____

We say "don't judge a book by its cover" but we all have a cover, an outer appearance that others see and make assumptions about. These assumptions may or may not be true. If you had to create a cover for the book of YOUR LIFE, what might it look like?

Please research some examples of "Altered Books" and sketch or write down some ideas you think you might be able to use.

9 Important Things

What are the 9 most important things to you? They can be real things like a dog or a person, or a feeling like love, or freedom. What are the 9 things you do not want to live without? Write each one in a box below, and draw a simple symbol for each. If nature was important to you, you could draw a leaf.

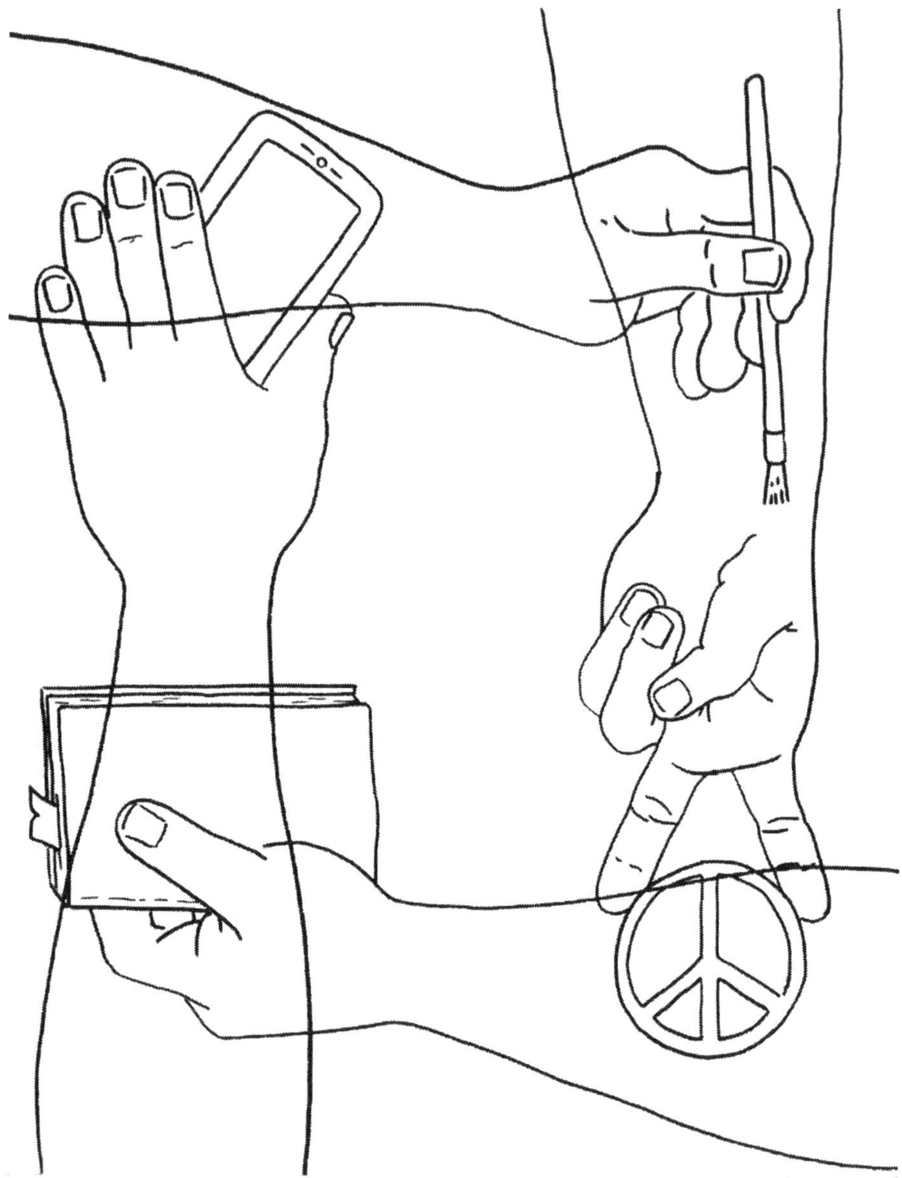

Hands We use objects and symbols every day. Trace your hands 4 times, overlapping, then go back in and fill in simple details like nails and main wrinkles. Be sure to include 4 important symbols that relate to you or the things you value.

Consider what you will put in the center. Will you overlap letters of your name, create a single important symbol or do a self portrait? It's up to you.

Where lines overlap making new shapes, color in each shape a different color. This is a great time to learn to blend colors. Try using only primary colors and have white available as a bonus color. Because our lines are black, black color is not an option for this project.

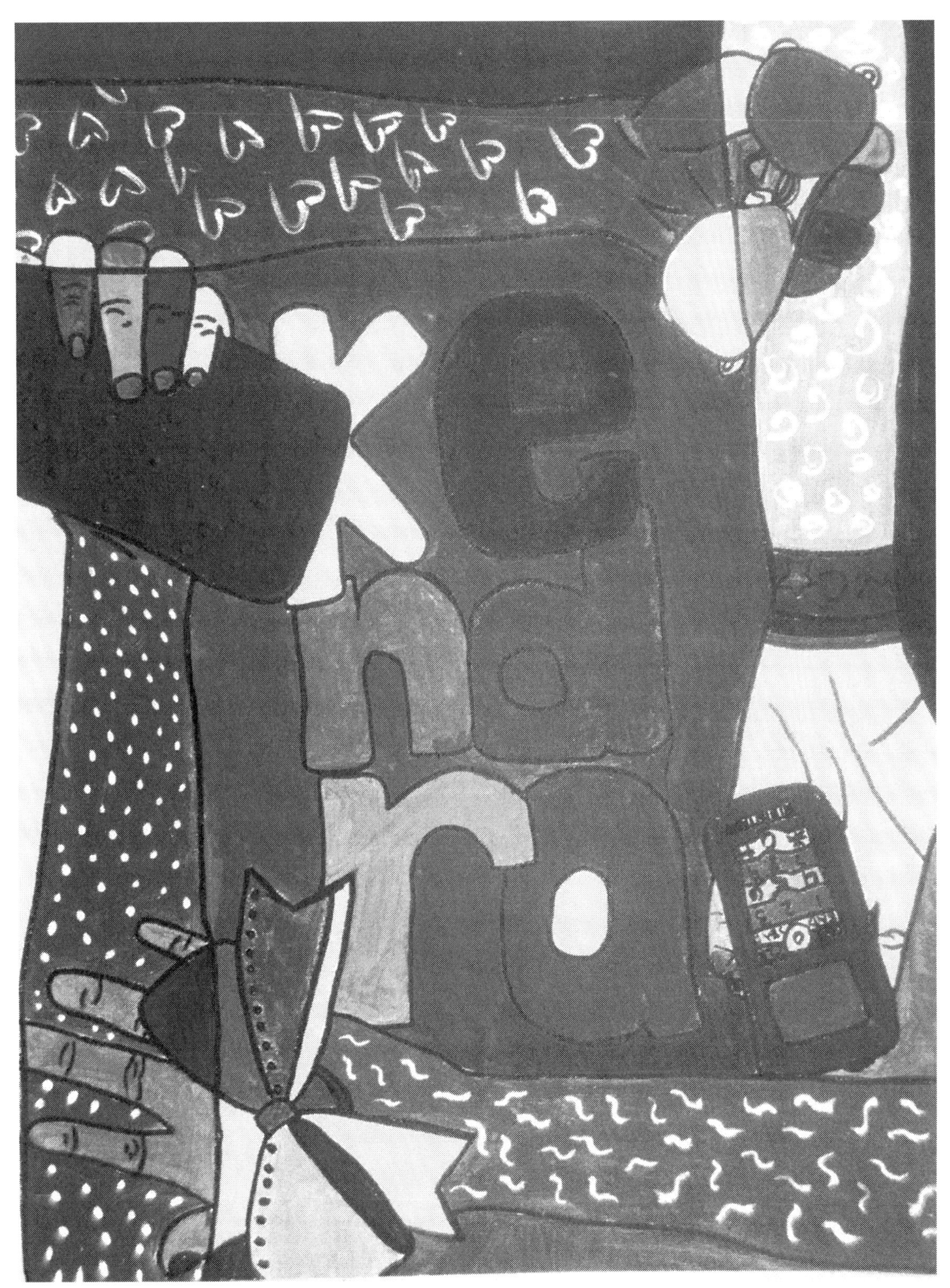

This sample is not in the student edition

Masks

Masks are usually used to hide the identity of the wearer. However, in this project, we are going to design a mask that will show others a side of you that you normally keep hidden from others, or something people don't normally know about you. This can be done through using symbols and shapes that you can either paint on the mask, or shape the mask to look like. So, if people assume you are kind of "ditzy" but you're really smart, you can shape the mask into the shape of an owl to represent how smart you are.

1. Sketch out how you want your mask to look including any symbols that you might paint on to the mask. Also, write down the meaning of your symbols as a reminder for yourself if you have a number of symbols that you are painting unto the mask.

> REMEMBER: This can be a mask that can be worn OR a mask that is simply decoration on a wall. You should decide what kind it will be before you begin , so you'll know how to build it.

2. We will create a foam base and build up the features on the face. Aluminum foil works too. WARNING: Carving foam is VERY messy. So is plaster work. YOU are responsible for YOUR area. No one will be allowed to sit in alternative seats for this project. If someone irresponsible sits near you… you may become responsible for their mess in your space.

3. After carving the foam, you'll plaster it. After it dries, you can begin to paint and add materials like feathers or other objects to the mask. You may want to bring some craft items from home if you do not have them here.

The student edition has a sketch page next →

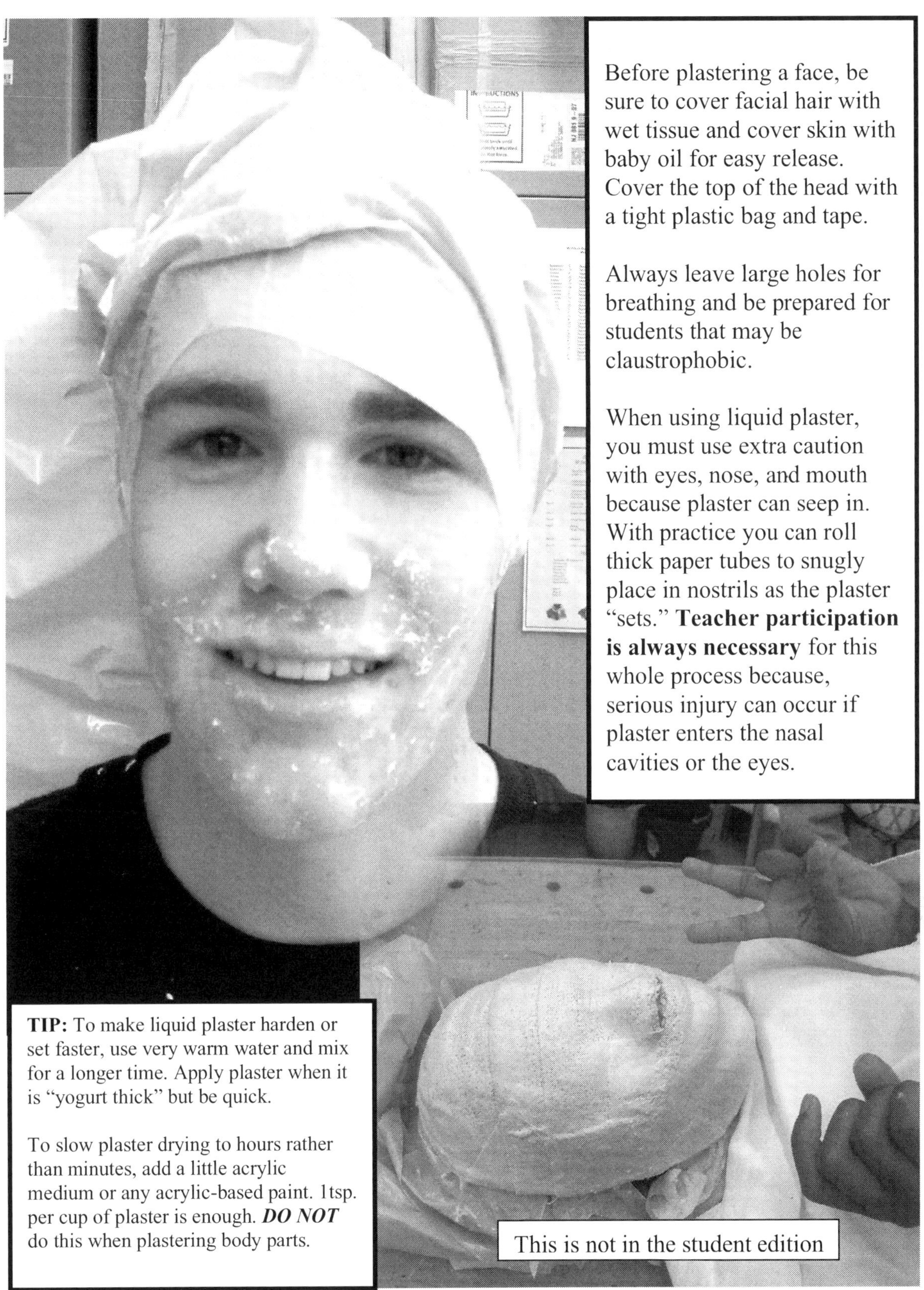

Before plastering a face, be sure to cover facial hair with wet tissue and cover skin with baby oil for easy release. Cover the top of the head with a tight plastic bag and tape.

Always leave large holes for breathing and be prepared for students that may be claustrophobic.

When using liquid plaster, you must use extra caution with eyes, nose, and mouth because plaster can seep in. With practice you can roll thick paper tubes to snugly place in nostrils as the plaster "sets." **Teacher participation is always necessary** for this whole process because, serious injury can occur if plaster enters the nasal cavities or the eyes.

TIP: To make liquid plaster harden or set faster, use very warm water and mix for a longer time. Apply plaster when it is "yogurt thick" but be quick.

To slow plaster drying to hours rather than minutes, add a little acrylic medium or any acrylic-based paint. 1tsp. per cup of plaster is enough. ***DO NOT*** do this when plastering body parts.

This is not in the student edition

Who Am I?

Often outward perceptions are different from reality. For example, people may know you like art, but may not know you traveled internationally. You may use visual codes to hide information you do not really want to share with others. We will use these lists to come up with an expressive work of art.

What I know about myself	**How the world sees me <u>or</u> how I see the world, <u>or</u> how I see my future.**
1. ____________________	1. ____________________
2. ____________________	2. ____________________
3. ____________________	3. ____________________
4. ____________________	4. ____________________
5. ____________________	5. ____________________
6. ____________________	6. ____________________
7. ____________________	7. ____________________
8. ____________________	8. ____________________
9. ____________________	9. ____________________
10. ____________________	10. ____________________
11. ____________________	11. ____________________
12. ____________________	12. ____________________

How might you use art to express what you have written about above? Could it be an altered book with one kind of cover and different inside pages? Perhaps a silhouette with what you know about yourself inside and the other list on the outside... Maybe a box showing the differences inside and out. Start with a sketch on the next page for ideas.

Student edition has a sketch page

Teacher Resource: https://youtu.be/DI_2bUbFcgA and https://bit.ly/insideboxes

Memorial Project

We will be creating an artwork based on someone special to you who is *no longer around you*. This could be through a death, but also because they may have moved, lost contact, or a separation because of a divorce. If you have not lost someone in your life, please pick someone you admire who is not living.

For privacy, if you prefer, you may use the person's initials to write below.
Their name is: ______________________

Write about your most vivid memory of this person.

____

____

____

____

What about him or her has changed your life?

____

____

____

If you could tell people only one thing about this person, what would you say?

____

____

Please write 5 positive words describing the person.

____

Did he or she have any shortcomings, negative traits? Mention 1 or 2 of them.

____

The student edition has a sketch page next →

This memorial is about the student's grandfather and their long road trips to the ocean. This is their van riding a wave, symbolizing the fun of the experience.

This page is not in the student edition.

Exploration of Culture:

What is *Culture*? The customs, arts, social institutions, and heritage of a particular nation, people, or other social group. What is/are your cultures?

_______________,__ ______________, ________________, _______________

Artists like Romare Bearden and others often tie their culture into their artwork to connect to a larger community.

- Write about an event that shaped who you are: positive or negative?
- What do you celebrate culturally, as part of a larger community?
- Part of being _______________ means_____________.
- The best part of being ____________ is ___________________.
- _____________ is a cultural hero for __________ because ________.

____

____

____

____

____

____

____

____

____

Sketch on the next page a scene that helps illustrate some or all of your writing.

Idiom Project

An idiom is a phrase, when taken as a whole, has a meaning different from the meanings of the individual words. Idioms can be cultural or specific to a language or community. The phrase *"raining cats and dogs"* is an example of an idiom. English speakers understand that this doesn't refer to domesticated animals at all, but that it describes very intense rain.

Based on your own cultural background(s), look up 3 idioms and record them below. Pick one to illustrate on the next page.

Culture: ______________________________

Idiom: ____

____

____

Translation: ____

____

Culture: ______________________________

Idiom: ____

____

____

Translation: ____

____

Culture: ______________________________

Idiom: ____

____

____

Translation: ____

____

Unsung Heroes

1. Five richest people in the world.
a.______________________________
b.______________________________
c. ______________________________
d.______________________________
e. ______________________________

2. Five sports trophy winners.
a.______________________________
b.______________________________
c. ______________________________
d.______________________________
e. ______________________________

3. Last five winners of Miss America.
a.______________________________
b.______________________________
c. ______________________________
d.______________________________
e. ______________________________

4. 5 people who have won the Nobel prize.
a.______________________________
b.______________________________
c. ______________________________
d.______________________________
e. ______________________________

5. Five Academy Award winners.
a.______________________________
b.______________________________
c. ______________________________
d.______________________________
e. ______________________________

1. 5 teachers who were good to you.
a.______________________________
b.______________________________
c. ______________________________
d.______________________________
e. ______________________________

2. 5 people who have helped you through a difficult time.
a.______________________________
b.______________________________
c. ______________________________
d.______________________________
e. ______________________________

3. 5 people you would share your lottery winnings with.
a.______________________________
b.______________________________
c. ______________________________
d.______________________________
e. ______________________________

4. 5 people you miss in your life.
a.______________________________
b.______________________________
c. ______________________________
d.______________________________
e. ______________________________

5. 5 of the kindest people you know.
a.______________________________
b.______________________________
c. ______________________________
d.______________________________
e. ______________________________

Which list was easier to create? ____

Who appears on your lists the most? ____

Why are they so special to you? ____

____

____

What kind of artwork could you make to honor that person's influence?

Printmaking Experience

1. What kind of printmaking did you explore?

____

____

2. Describe the process:

____

____

____

____

____

____

3. Name a famous artist who also did this.

____

4. What was most challenging for you?

____

____

____

5. What was most successful for you?

____

____

____

____

Printmaking Vocabulary

1. Brayer: A small, hand-held rubber roller used to spread printing ink evenly on a surface before printing.

2. Block/Plate: A piece flat material, with a design on its surface, used to print repeated impressions of that design. Called a PLATE in etching and engraving.

3. Printmaking: The process of designing and producing prints using a printing block, woodcut, etching, screen-printing, etc.

4. Edition: A set of identical/similar prints, that are numbered and signed. This set of prints have been pulled by or under the supervision of the artist.

5. Registration: Adjustment of separate plates/blocks, or paper in color printing to ensure correct alignment of the colors.

6. Burnishing: Rubbing the back of printing paper on an inked block/plate to make a print.

7. Monoprint: A print made as an edition of one. It is an image painted on glass or plexi-glass, and transferred (or stamped) onto paper. Each single print is unique.

8. Printing Press: A device used by a fine art printmaker to produce prints one copy at a time. It applies pressure between a sheet of paper and an inked printing plate.

9. Proof: Trial prints done to check the status of the work.

10. Prints: A process to transfer an image to another surface. Copies of an original artwork.

Music: Resource https://www.artedguru.com/home/music-as-a-bridge

1. My favorite song right now is ________________________ by ____________________

2. I like it so much because

____

____

Music can "speak' to us, just as art can. Music can stir emotions of all kinds from joy, and excitement, to sadness, and pain, to even emotions of anger and inspiring people to take action!

3. A song that I like, that might surprise people is : __________________ by ________________

4. It reminds me of ____

____

5. A song that makes me feel sad is : ____________________________ by ________________

6. It reminds me of ____

____

7. A song that I like that gives me hope or joy is : ___________________ by ________________

8. This is because: ____

____

Highlight the one above you feel has the most visual imagery. (Like you could *draw* it.)

Find the lyrics of the song on an iPad or your phone, and write just 1 paragraph from the song below. If the song includes words that are inappropriate for school, add a black space.

____

____

____

____

____

Alphabet Themes

Video Support: https://youtu.be/3dnoaVsAkJQ

LIST 5 themes for yourself and 3 themes of those close to you (Mom, Dad…)
BROAD themes are better than focused ones. You will have more choices.
For instance, choosing *Field Hockey* limits the amount of imagery you can use, but if your theme was *Sports* then you would have tons of other stuff to incorporate.

— Instead of Clothes, choose fashion (Then you can include Fashion Logos)
— Instead of Vegetables, choose Foods
— Instead of Rock and Roll, choose Music

There are 3 levels of difficulty to this project.

Level 1: A Single object repeated to create a whole alphabet, like the balloons below. If done very well can get a high potential grade of a low "A."

Level 2: A single concept with 30% to 60% related original ideas thrown in, like a theme of Plants. If done very well can get a high potential grade of a mid-range "A."

Level 3: Every letter is a different image within the theme. This is the most difficult and potentially can get the highest grade of 100%. (Here is a Logo Alphabet)

*****The Letters do not have to coordinate with the meaning. "A" does not have to be "APPLE" the symbol just has to be an "A" SHAPE.*****

Holiday Themed Alphabet Sample

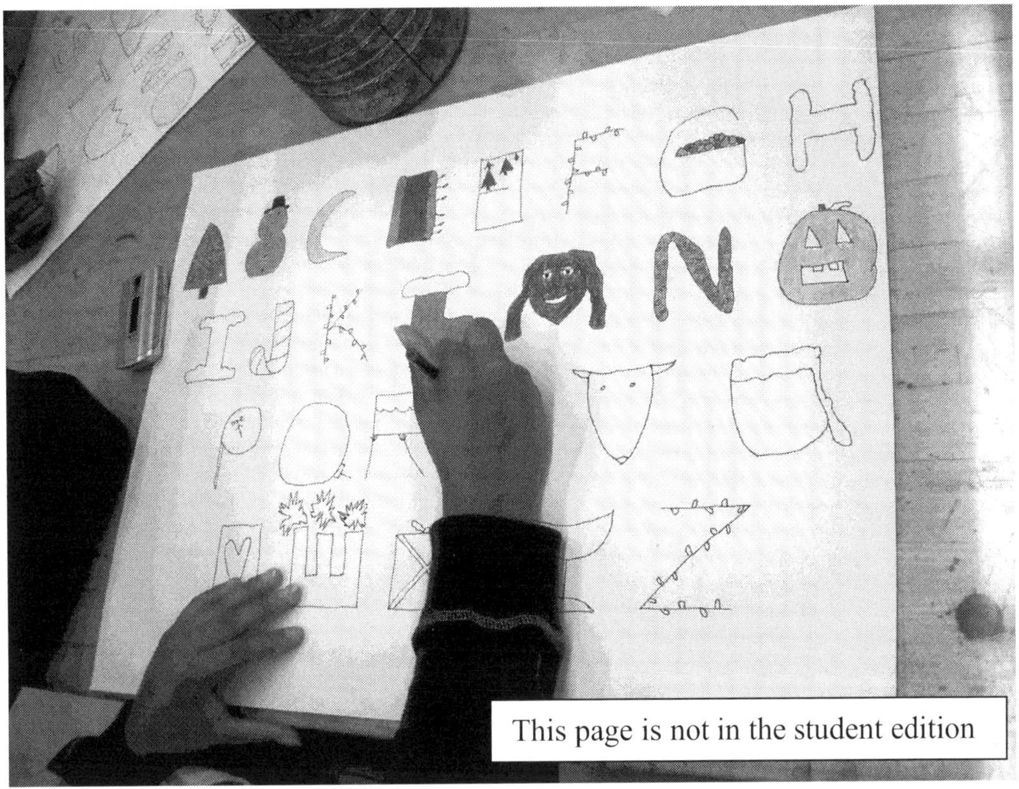

This page is not in the student edition

Note how each letter is different but still follows this student's theme of holidays.
Tutorial: https://youtu.be/3dnoaVsAkJQ

By choosing a theme students can even make sculptural words to express their meaning.

Helpful Hints

DO NOT START WITH "A"

Start with the easiest ideas and cross them off. If you chose SPORTS, make a ball and cross off the "O" first! Use the alphabet below to cross off what you have sketched. Tutorial: https://youtu.be/3dnoaVsAkJQ

REMEMBER! Letters can look many different ways and still be that letter.

A a A a A A a

Cross off letters as you sketch them.

A B C D E F G H

I J K L M N O

P Q R S T U

V W X Y Z

What is your theme? ____

Alphabet Sketch Page

Name Illustration Project

Name ______________________________ Period _____ Date: _________

What is the name of your client? ______________________________

Have them check the spelling.

What is your job? ______________________________

What are your hobbies? ______________________________

____

Do you have a special talent? ______________________________

What is your favorite song/musical artist. ______________________________

What is your favorite movie or TV Show. ______________________________

Do you have any pets? (If so, what kind) ______________________________

____

What is your favorite food? ______________________________

What is your favorite snack? ______________________________

What is your birth month? ______________________________

Do you have any collections? ______________________________

When you were a child, what did you want to be when you grew up?

____

Initial Sketch Below: *(Student workbook includes a blank page for sketching)*

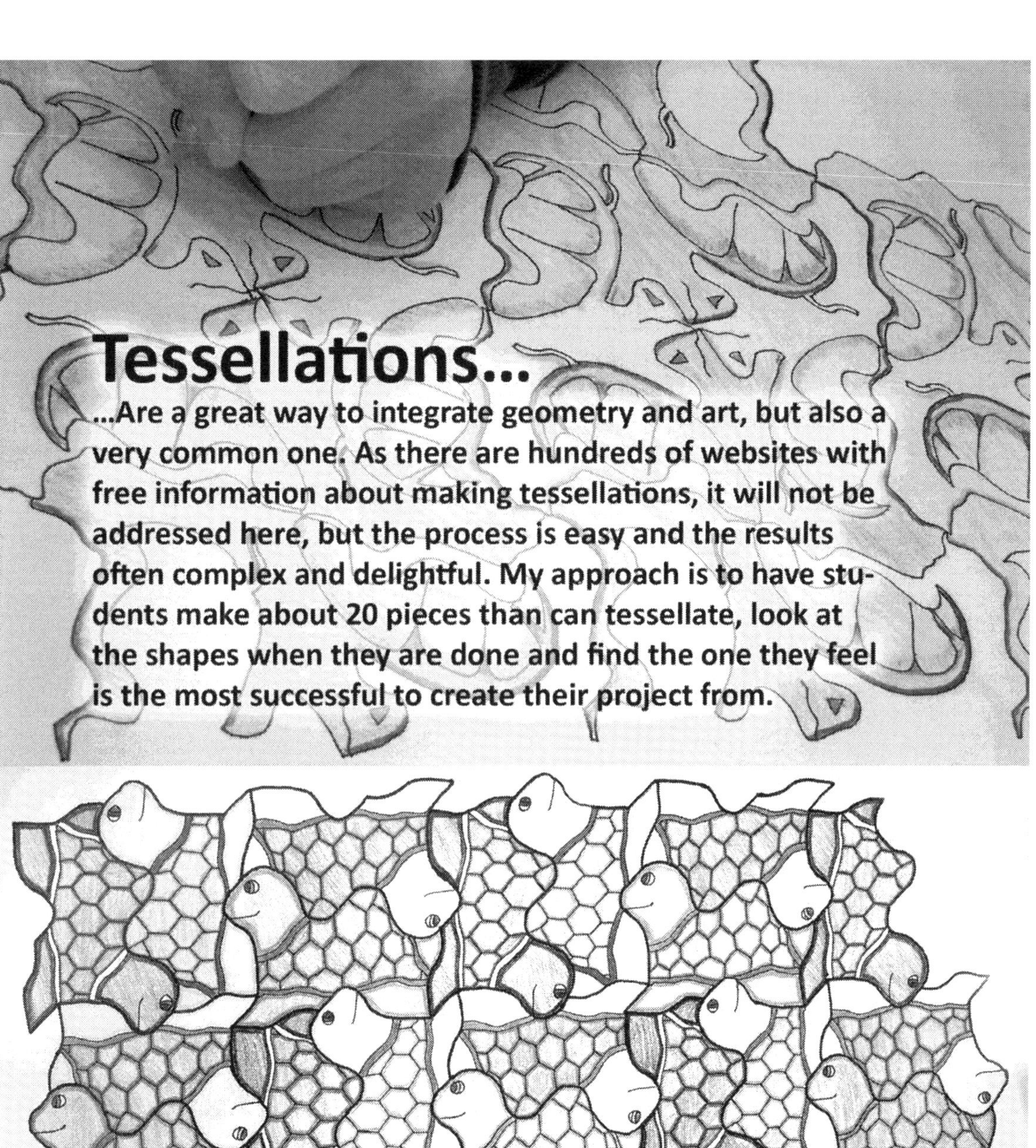

Tessellations...

...Are a great way to integrate geometry and art, but also a very common one. As there are hundreds of websites with free information about making tessellations, it will not be addressed here, but the process is easy and the results often complex and delightful. My approach is to have students make about 20 pieces than can tessellate, look at the shapes when they are done and find the one they feel is the most successful to create their project from.

This page not in the student edition.
Tutorials: https://bit.ly/tessL8

Treasure Maps: Resource at www.artedguru.com/home/cartography-exploration

Create a treasure map of an imaginary island. The island can take on the contour of an object, but break it into small pieces so it is not too obvious. Include the following: Detailed border, rose compass, longitude, latitude, 5 land feature symbols, key for symbols, 2 landmarks, 2 water symbols in the water, 1 sea monster, and 1 ship. Maps can be aged by wrinkling and soaking in coffee. Include geology & cartography elements.

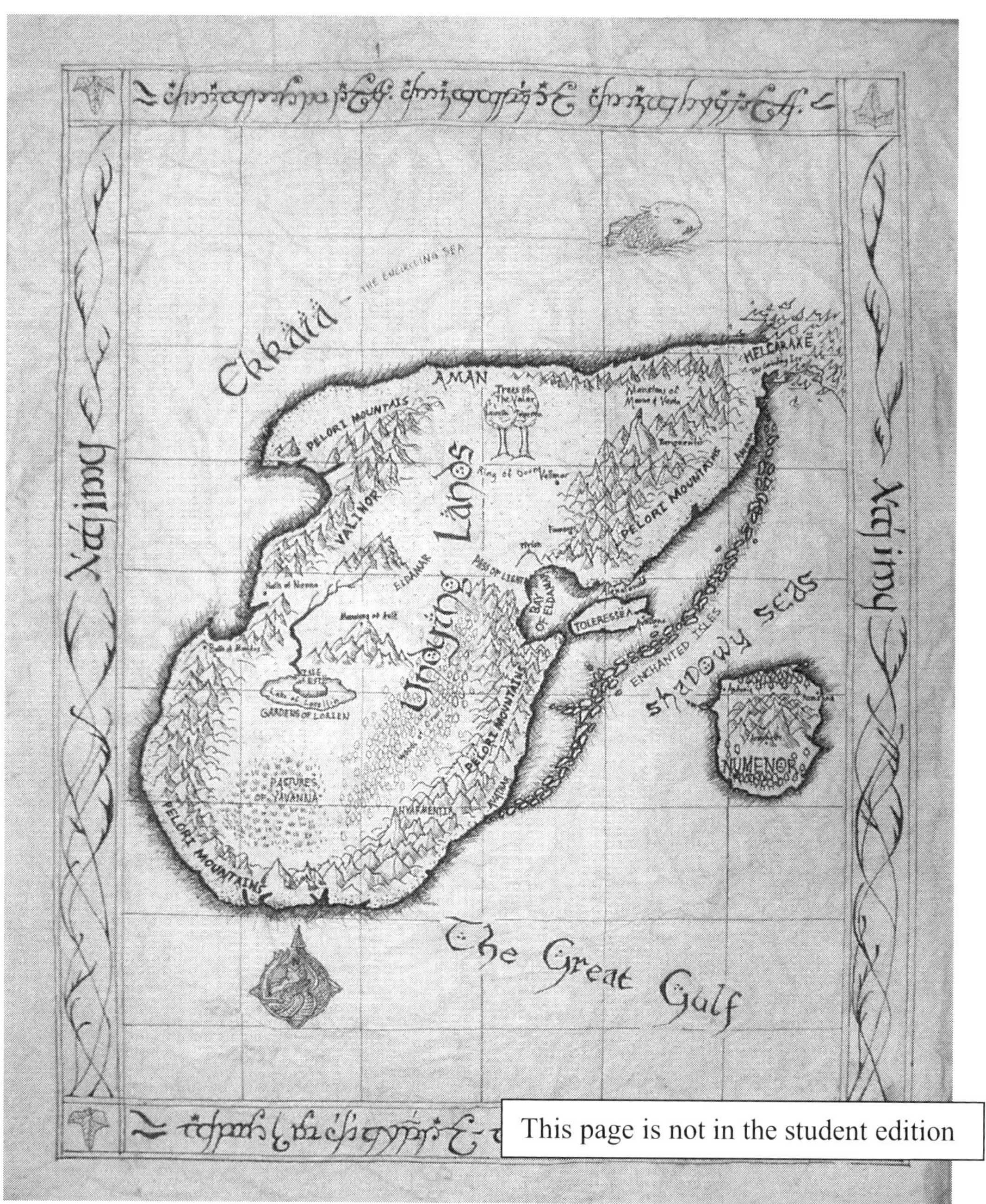

This page is not in the student edition

Grids

Grids can be a great way to transform a design, enlarge or reduce a drawing. They are often used to make murals. Tutorial: https://youtu.be/eTfSt7HYYXg

The following pages have 3 grids of different scale. You can place a piece of plastic, acetate, or overhead sheet on top of the grid and trace the lines using a ruler and sharpie marker to have your own grid. It can be placed over a photograph, magazine image, etc, and transferred to a similar grid on another paper.

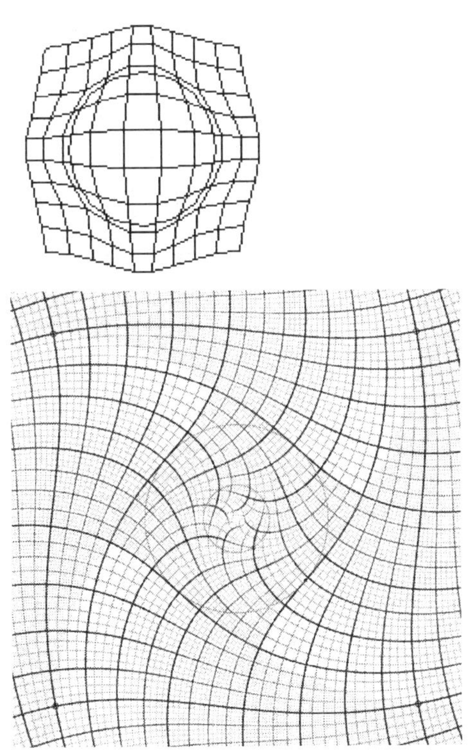

Sometimes it is fun to create a "*warped*" grid that has waves in it and curves and transfer the design into it to create a surrealistic or altered transfer.

When doing a warped grid, put a regular grid on top of an image, and then create a warped grid the image will be transferred to.

With the warped grid, straight lines are not necessary. It is sometimes best to make the outside border and divide that shape in half, and each subsequent division in half again until the grid has the number of divisions you feel will work. This can be done by hand with visual estimates.

Tutorial: https://youtu.be/fqIhUZ0seX8

Take your time and go square-by-square to transfer your design.

The regular gridding technique is very old and we know it was used by many Renaissance artists like Leonardo da Vinci.

This is a famous portrait by Chuck Close, re-made on a warped grid. If students have access to Photoshop, they can alter pictures there and draw based on the printout.

Improvements with Regular Gridding Technique

Students with low skills can do well…

This page is not in the student edition

Art and Economics

What is the economy? ____

____

____

Though a career in art can be both creative and rewarding, some fields are more susceptible to the economy than others. Careers like teaching are often more stable than working in an advertising and design company. Schools need teachers, there will always be children, but when the economy gets bad, or the flow of money is less, companies spend less on things like advertising. Employees have less money to spend on things like art, going to museums, seeing movies, or even art therapy.

Even an art teacher can lose his or her job if a school feels that art just is not as important as other subjects and school budgets are being tightened.

Art is often seen of as a luxury, so often the first financial hardships are felt by art galleries and the artists they represent. From 2007 through 2011, many galleries all over the world closed after being open for many generations. This was a result of the financial problems not only in the USA but all over the world.

Your teacher can show you a chart of the Dow Jones Industrial Average by going to Google → news → business and clicking on the Dow Jones link under the financial chart there.

In general, when this number rises, the economy is doing better than when it goes down. Daily ups and downs mean very little and can be changed by daily political events, but a month to month look at the Dow Jones Industrial Average can indicate if the economy is getting better or worse.

If unemployment is low and the economy is high, people are more likely to buy luxuries like jewelry, cars, homes or art.

In the last 30 days has the DOW gone up or down? ______________

In the last year has the DOW gone up or down? ______________

What is the current unemployment rate in your state and in the USA?

State: ____: ____________, USA: ____________ (Less than 6% is a sign of healthy employment)

Is the economy good now for art? ______________ Why do you think so? ______________

____

____

Would you guess things are getting better or worse? (And why?)______________________

____

____

Perspective

(1 Point, 2 Point, and 3 Point)

Vocabulary

— Perspective

— Horizon

— Vanishing Point

— Parallel

— Converging

— Vertical

— Eye Level

This is an example of 1 Point Perspective. Everything seems to be going to one point "A".

Your Name in 1 Point Perspective

Your Name in 1 Point Perspective

1. Can you draw your name with block letters? Do it below.
2. Create a horizon and vanishing point.
3. Make all corners of your name go to that vanishing point.
4. DO NOT draw lines that overlap the letters of your name.

Use a ruler and draw along all the edges that go into the background. Where do they meet? What do we call this point? Is it the same for the image below?

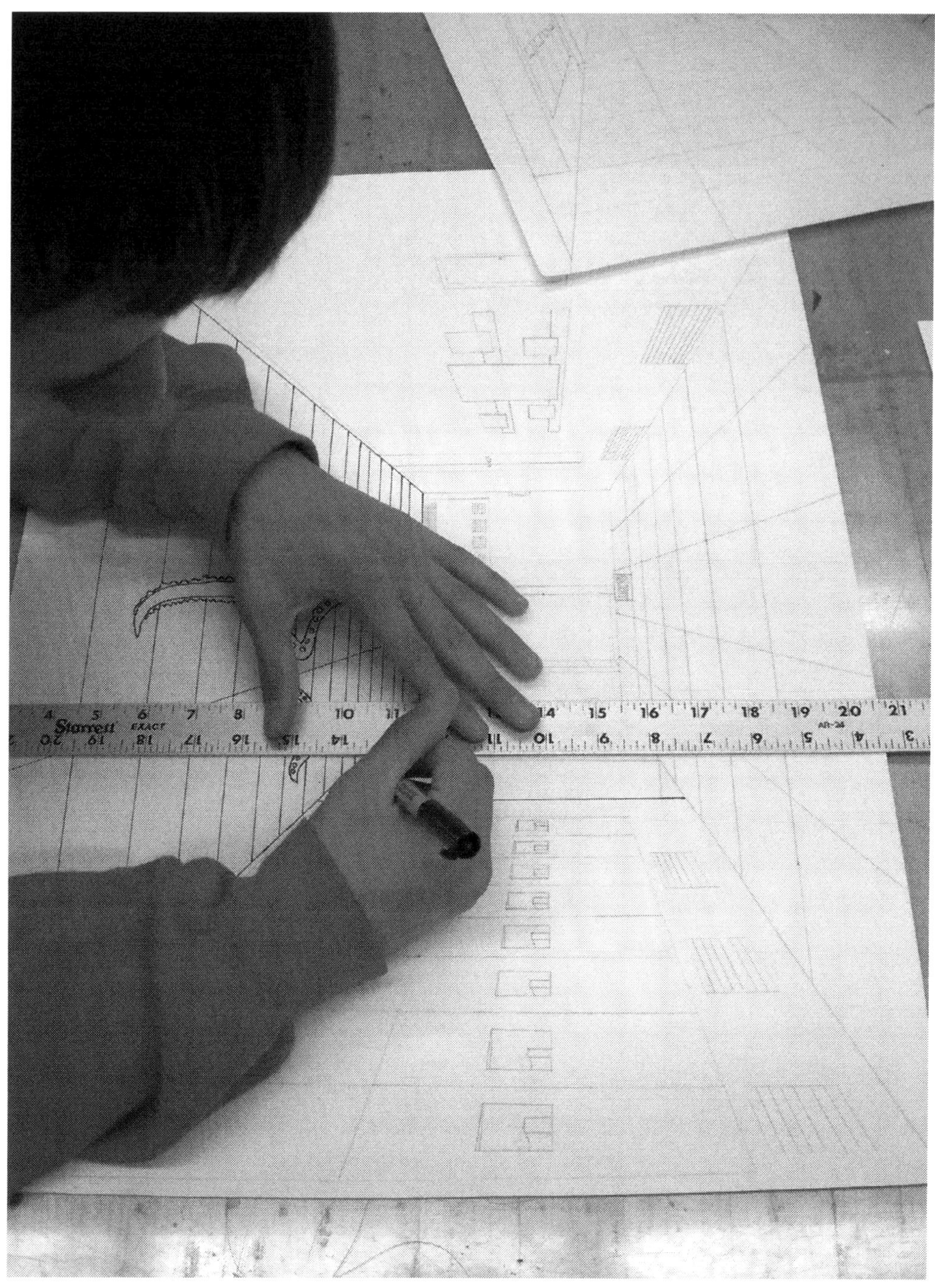

Students do a perspective drawing from observation of the school hallways, but finish by adding a surrealistic element. Here the student adds tentacles of some creature emerging from the floor.

Surreal school drawing samples in 1 Point Perspective.

By Ryan Orlofsky

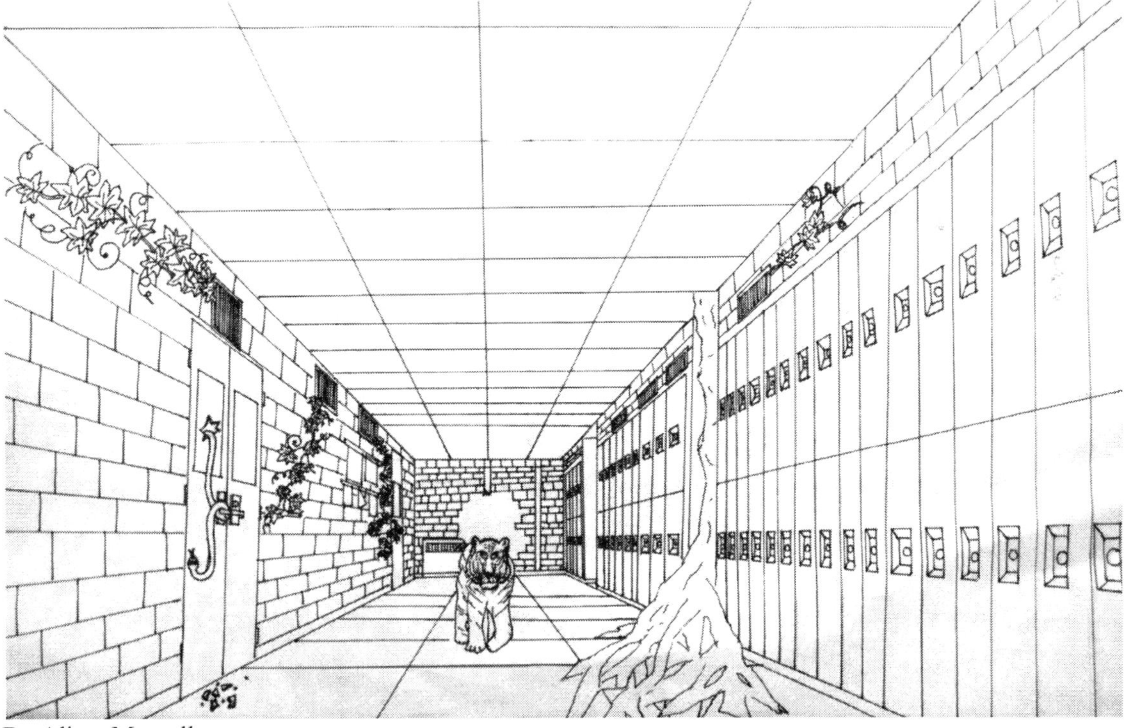

By Alissa Mazzella

This is an example of 2 Point Perspective. See how both sides seem to converge to different points on the same horizon.

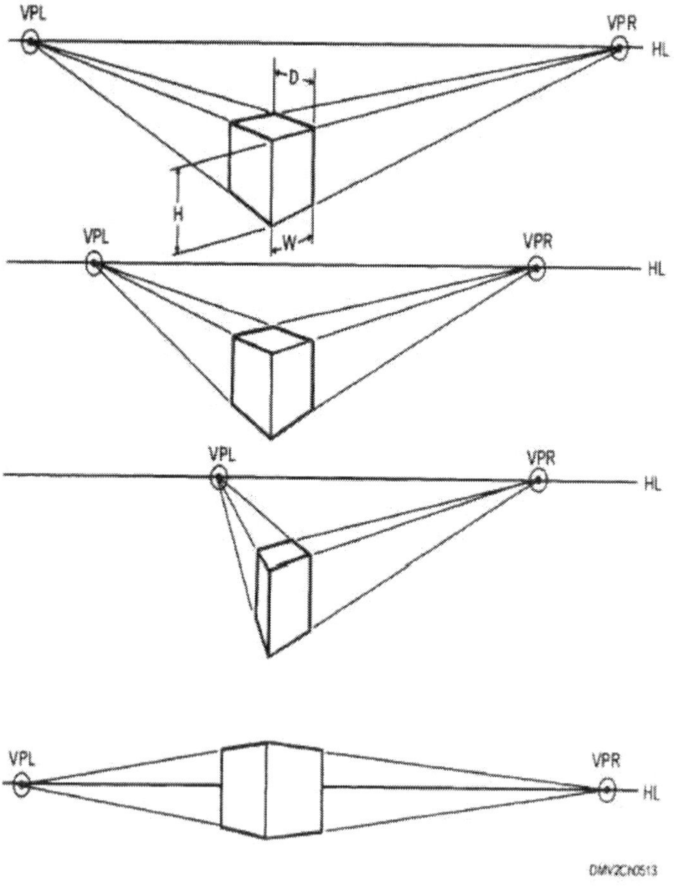

This is how 2 point perspective is used to draw boxes. You may not be required to do a 2 point perspective drawing, but you need to know about it and explain the concept.

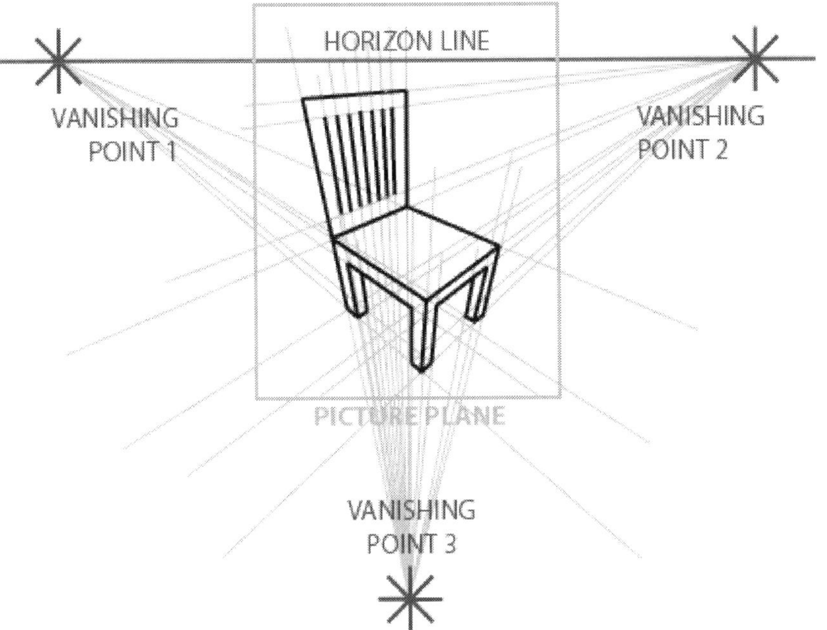

3 Point Perspective is shown above. It is NOT a requirement to do a project in 3 point perspective, but you do need to understand the concept.

Try to draw a cube below and make it look 3-D.

Drawing Boxes in 1 point perspective

1. Draw a horizontal line with a ruler, somewhere below. This is the *Horizon*. (It can cut through a box)
2. Draw a **dot** somewhere on the line.
3. Make the corners of the squares below connect to that **dot,** we'll call that the *Vanishing Point*.
4. Erase completely any lines that cut through a square.
5. Use parallel lines to show the back edge of each box.
6. Erase lines that go beyond the end of each box.

Student Edition contains 2 blank "Perspective Practice" pages.

Crosshatching

Repeated lines can create the illusion of shadow and form. The above image was done step by step to the right. This is the same technique used to create the faces you see on a dollar bill.

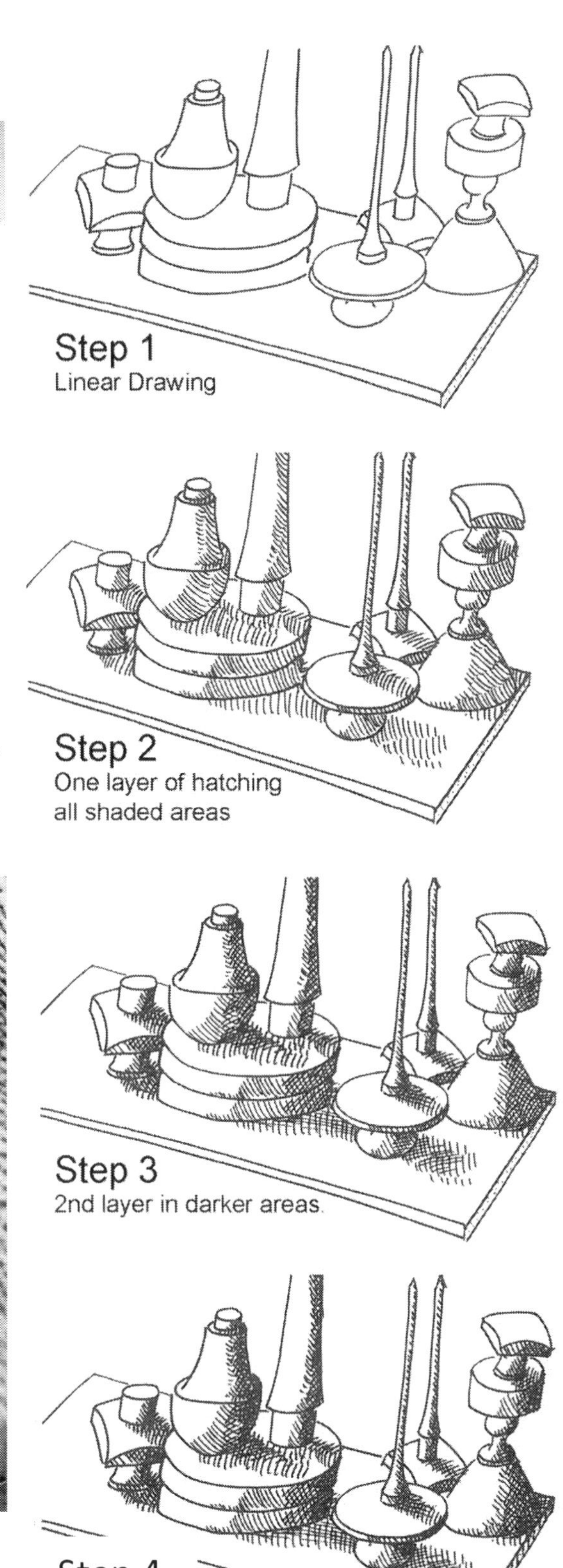

It can be done also with dots (Stippling) or any repeated line, even scribbles.

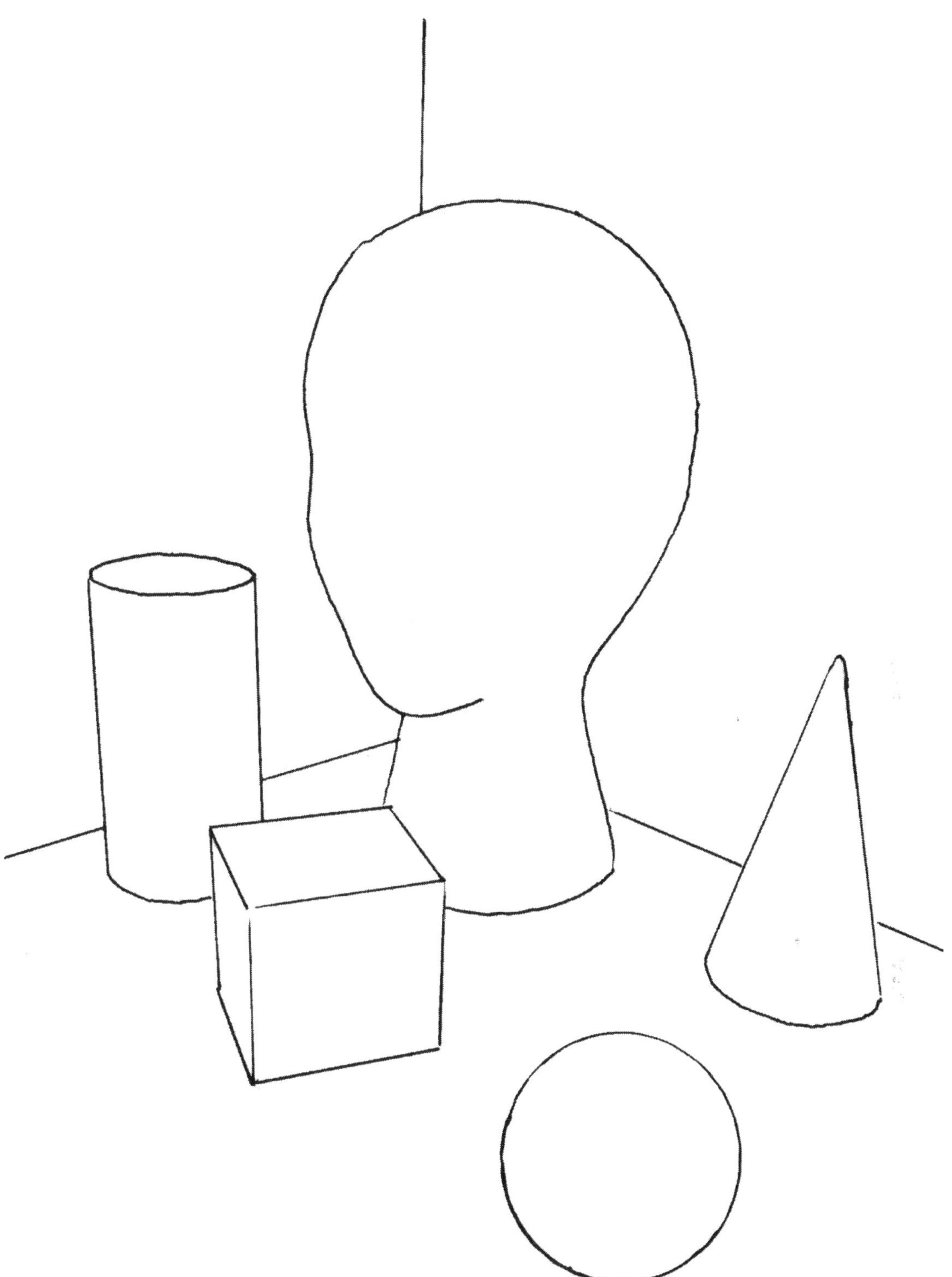

Practice your shading technique(s) above based on the photo on the left.

Coloring Spheres (Video Help: https://bit.ly/ColorSphere)

This first example is monochromatic (variation of a single color, like black or blue…)

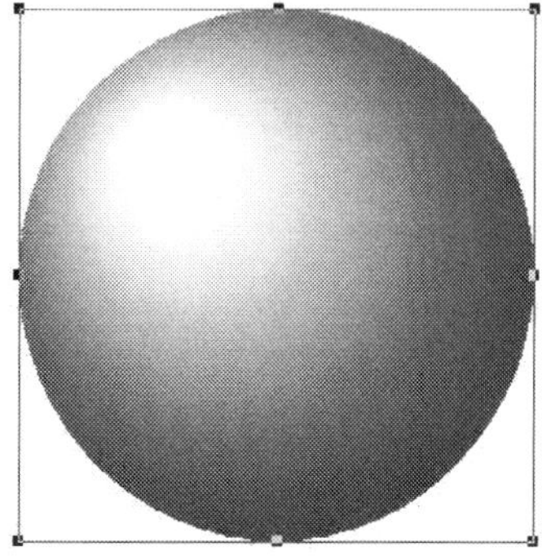

MONOCHROMATIC

Please color in the following 6 circles. See the sample so your circles look like shaded spheres too.

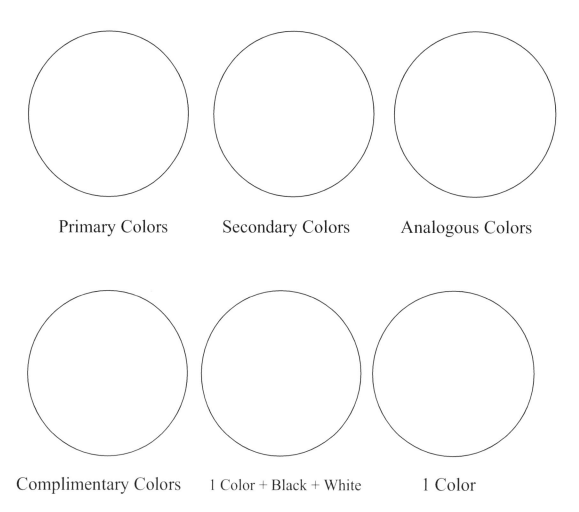

- Primary colors
- Secondary colors
- Analogous colors
- Complementary colors
- Any color plus black and white
- 1 color, use pressure to show light and dark.

Primary Colors

Secondary Colors

Analogous Colors

Complimentary Colors

1 Color + Black + White

1 Color

4 Basic Forms

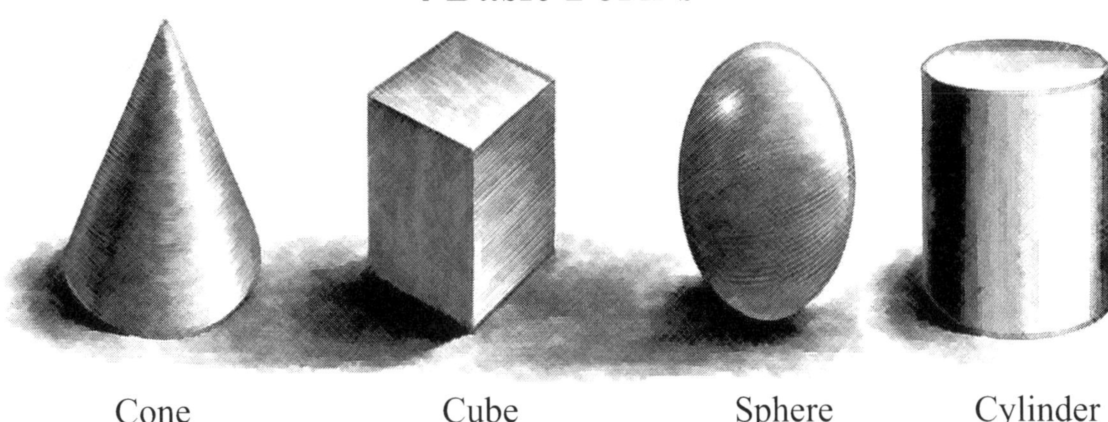

Cone　Cube　Sphere　Cylinder

Try drawing the 4 forms here. Color and shade them.

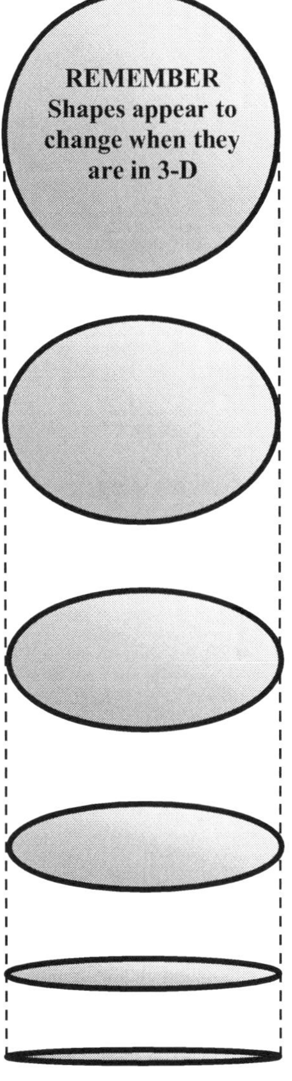

REMEMBER
Shapes appear to change when they are in 3-D

Face Proportions

Possible Lesson: https://bit.ly/SelfPortraits5

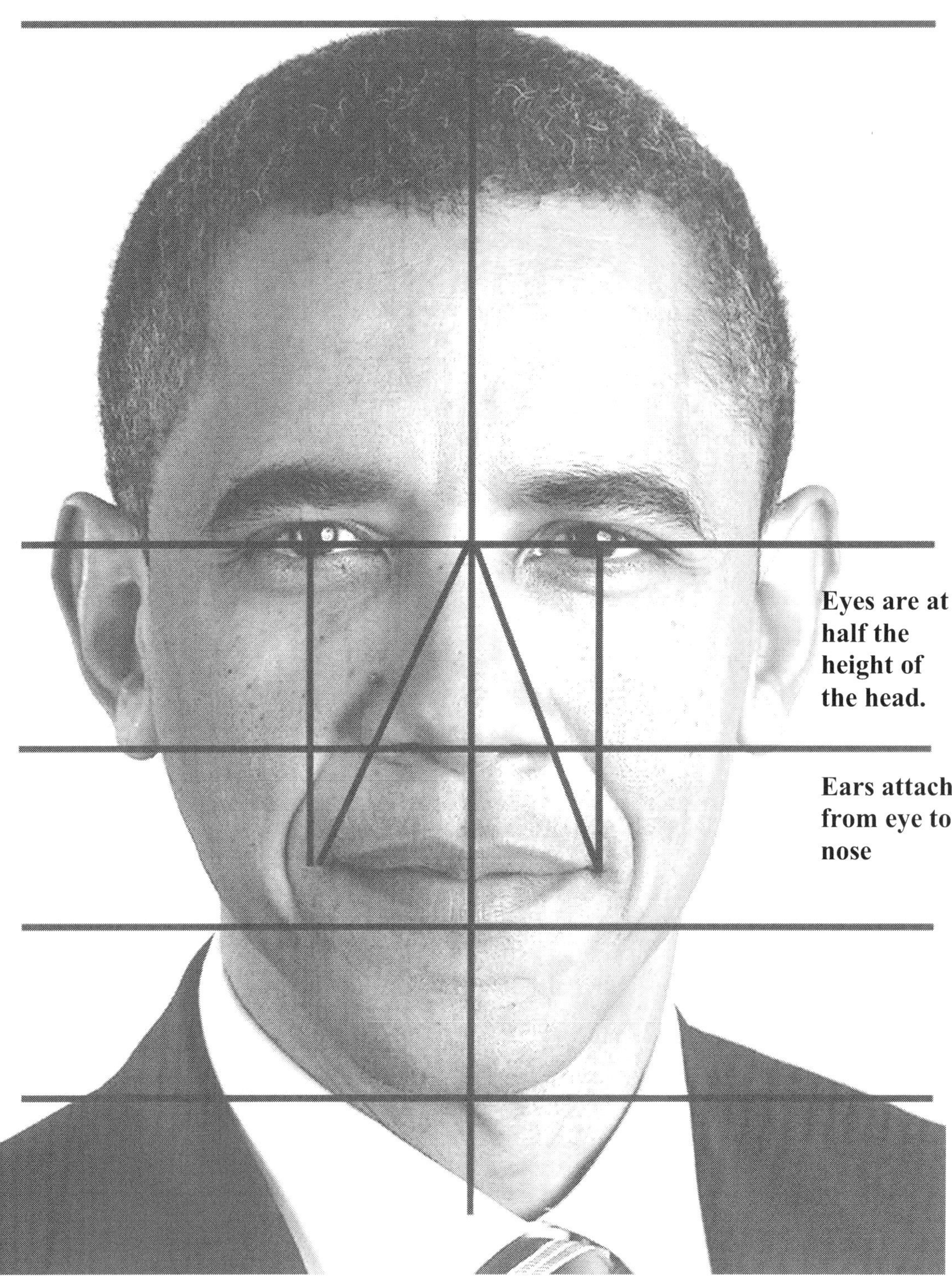

Eyes are at half the height of the head.
Ears attach from eye to nose

Face Map Proportions

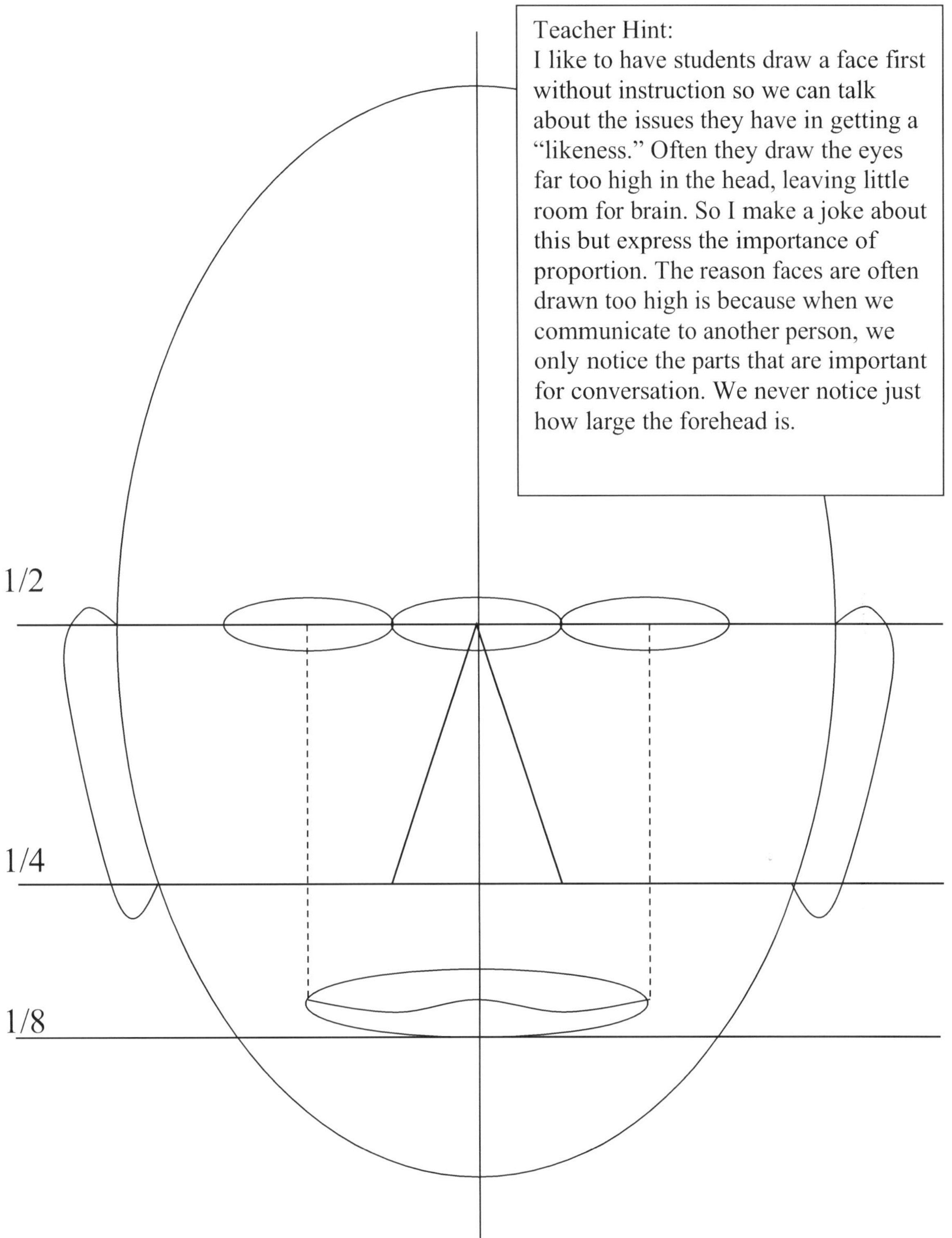

Teacher Hint:
I like to have students draw a face first without instruction so we can talk about the issues they have in getting a "likeness." Often they draw the eyes far too high in the head, leaving little room for brain. So I make a joke about this but express the importance of proportion. The reason faces are often drawn too high is because when we communicate to another person, we only notice the parts that are important for conversation. We never notice just how large the forehead is.

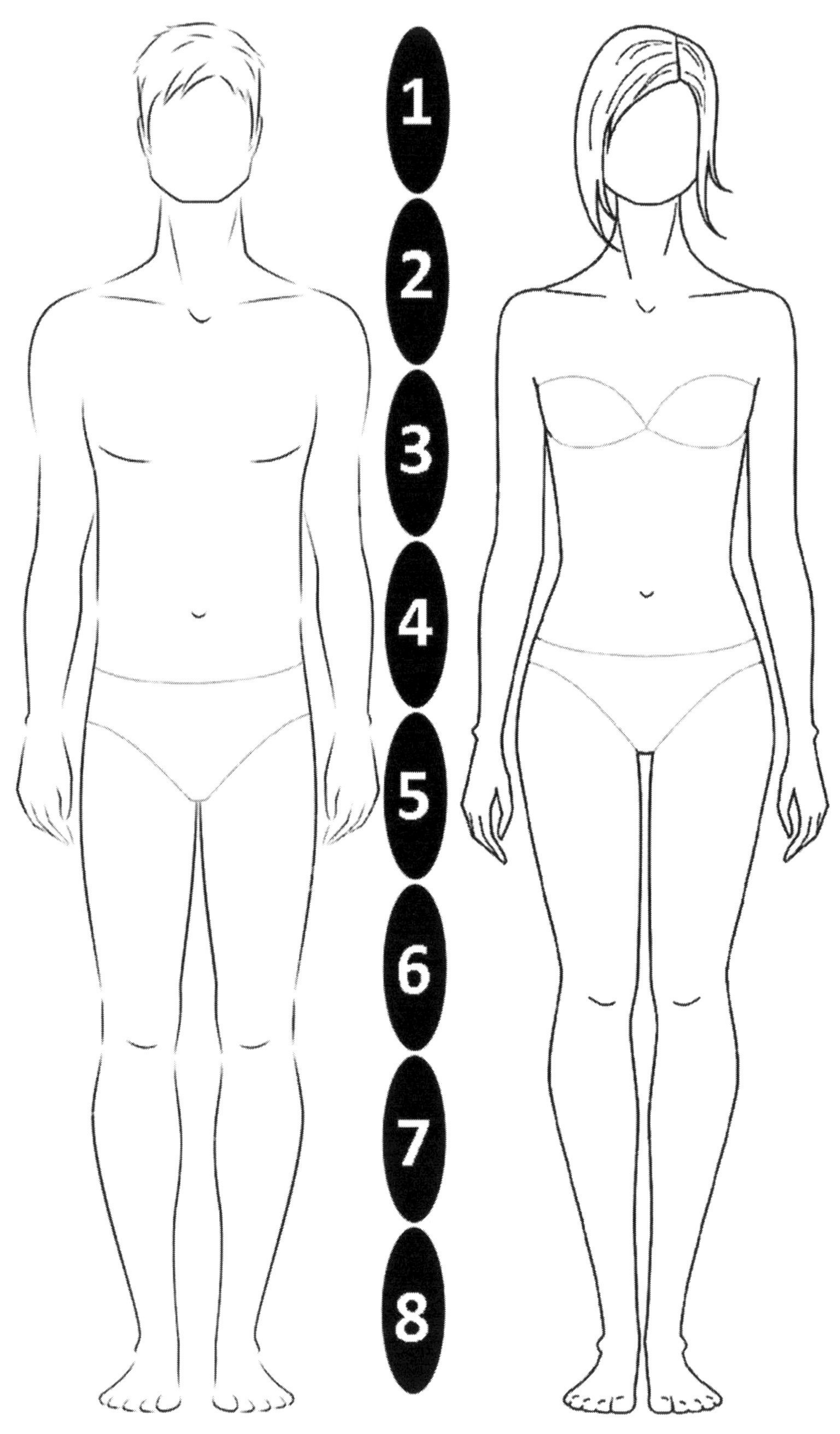
1
2
3
4
5
6
7
8

Fashion Unit:

Teacher Resource: https://youtu.be/mP-VsEmH5j4

Using these resources, you are to create 3 unique fashion designs. They must be based on human figure proportions of 8-Heads high. You may chose either male or female designs or switch them up.

You will create 3 designs:

- 1 Costume/uniform (Silly, fun, or serious)
- 1 formal (Evening gown, suit, wedding, something for a formal event)
- 1 of your personal fashion, something **YOU** might actually wear.

Before you begin, look through some magazines or other resources to find one or two items that will help inspire your 3 designs and unify them. So if you picked a Ferrari car, you might use the colors or elements for your designs, or do designs that are inspired by the ideas of speed.

Add your inspiration item(s) below:

Gesture Drawing:

To quickly catch the pose of a model in a few seconds or minutes we use gesture drawing. These are often done as a warm-up exercise for artists. Gesture drawing is not specific, but a quick general idea of the position. If done lightly, a final drawing can be worked on top of the gesture drawing. Take some times to do gesture drawings of your peers before you begin your final design. Practice making them 8-heads high.

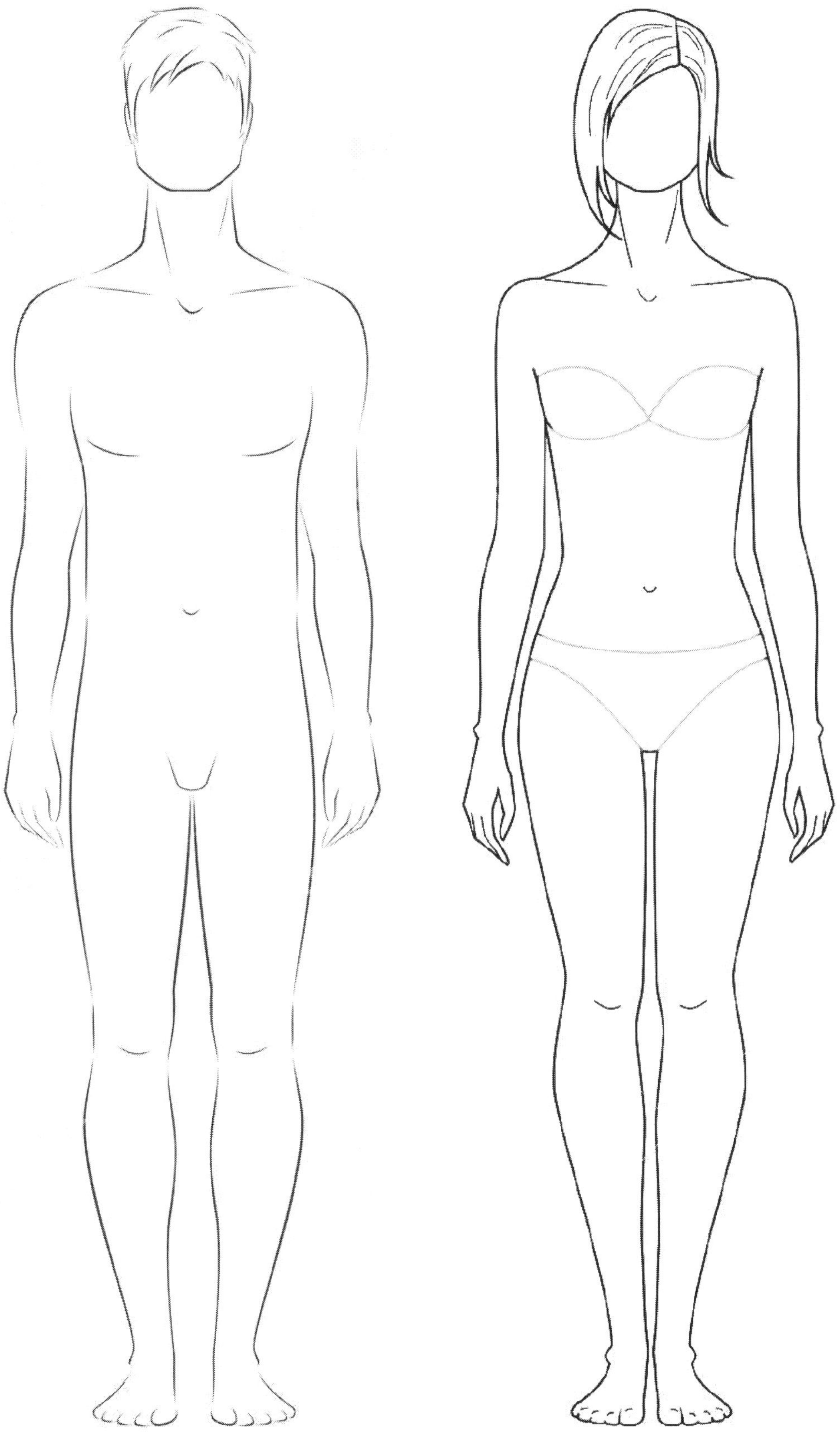

Sketch your fashion idea on top of these figures.

(Student edition has 3 of these pages)

Sculpture

Science Meets ART

In most cases diseases and illnesses are caused by a virus, parasite, abnormal cells, or infection. Name as many diseases or sicknesses that you can?

1.

2.

3.

4.

5.

6.

7.

8.

9.

10.

Choose one of the above illnesses. Look up what organism causes that illness, and what it looks like. Draw it below and add color too.

Your number _______ and its cause is ________________________________

Diseases and Other Creepy Crawlies

Find some time to go to the library or computer lab and look up viruses, bacteria and cancer cells. They can either print or sketch what they find. Below are Phages infecting a bacteria cell.

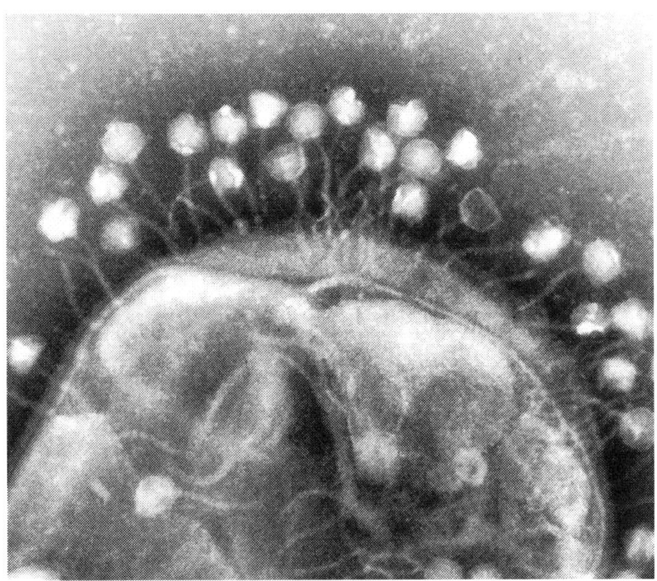

Above: *Mycobacteriophages*

TEACHER HINT:
I require my students to be able to find the proper scientific name for their cell, which later becomes the name of their project.

Students then re-create their cell with plaster over an aluminum foil base adding in straws, wire, dowels or pipe-cleaners to make it look as similar as possible.

When that is complete I ask them to finish their project with patterns, glitter, yarn, and artistic embellishments so that their work is not just clinical, but a work of sculptural art.

Virus Project Samples

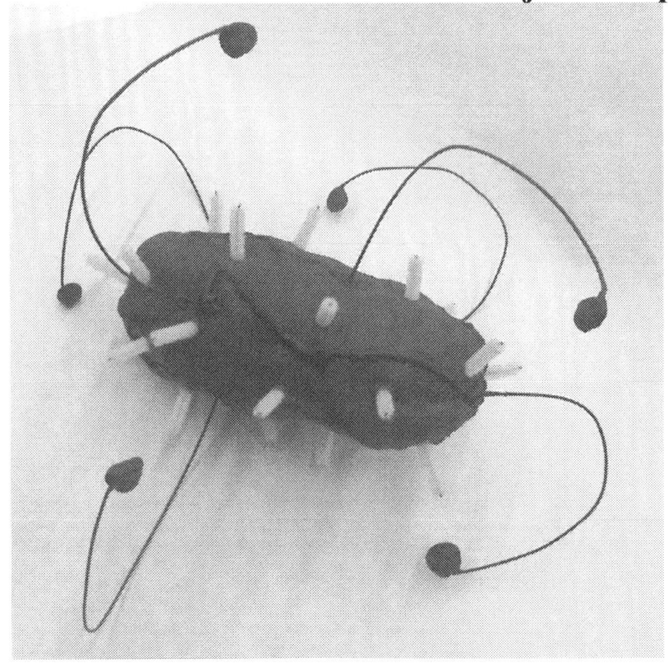

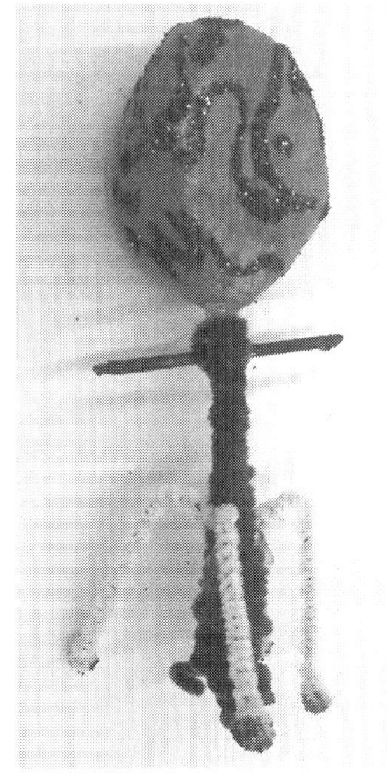

Sketch your project here:

Sculpting Wind   Video Support: https://bit.ly/5WindSculptures

What can wind symbolize?

1. ______________________ 2. ______________________

3. ______________________ 4. ______________________

5. ______________________ 6. ______________________

What kinds of things use wind for their form or function?

1. FLAGS ______________________ 2. ______________________

3. ______________________ 4. ______________________

5. ______________________ 6. ______________________

7. ______________________ 8. ______________________

9. ______________________ 10. ______________________

If you had to use wind in a sculpture to show your personality, what could you create?

____

____

____

____

____

See some examples of wind sculptures, and sketch what you might like to make below. Can you incorporate recycled materials like plastics, cans, etc?

Wind Sculpture Samples

https://youtu.be/f5pgGMMRMVc

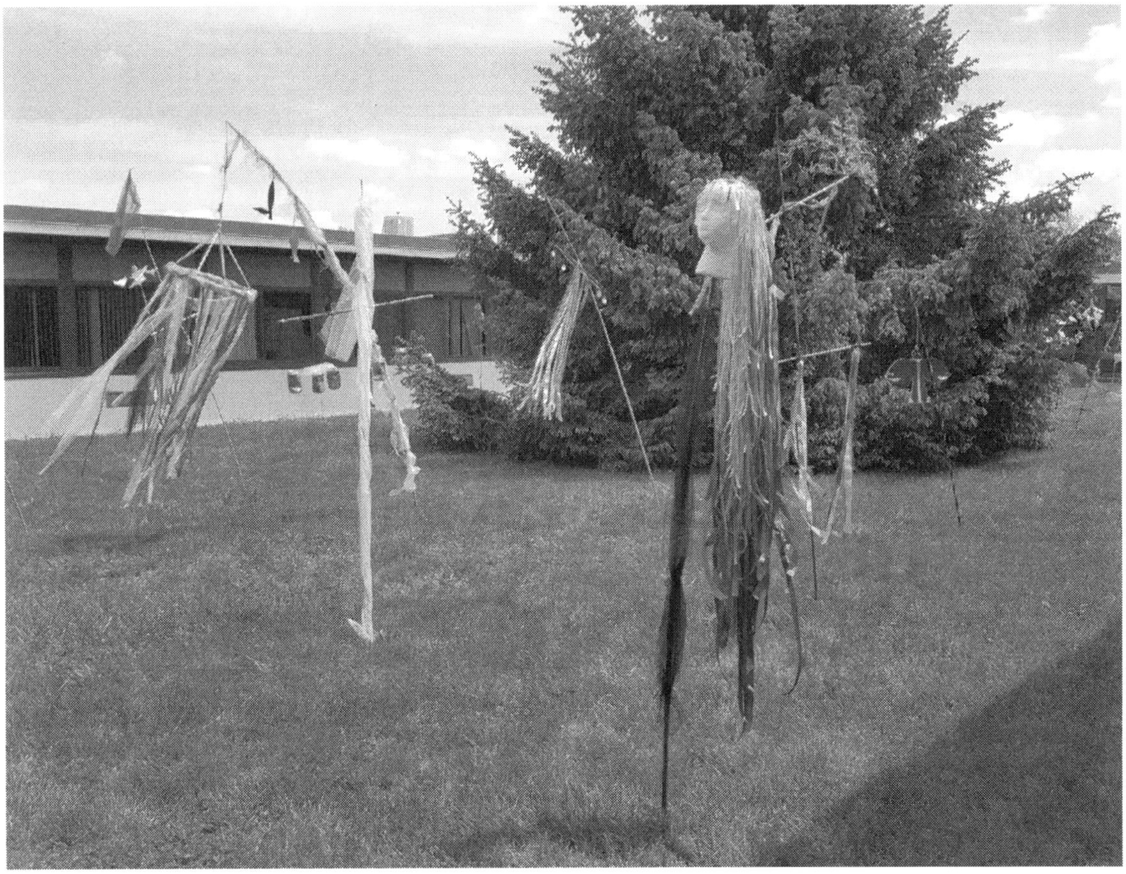

My Cultural Background

Create a project based on information on your cultural background by creating a background pattern of repeated pattern of cultural objects and a foreground animal representing that artist's personality. Many people have different cultural backgrounds.

Cultural Background #1 (Country of origin)	Cultural Background #2 (Country of origin)	Cultural Background #3 (Country of origin)
Cultural Objects *Flowers, crafts, trees, symbols*	Cultural Objects *Flowers, crafts, trees, symbols*	Cultural Objects *Flowers, crafts, trees, symbols*
Animals from that country	Animals from that country	Animals from that country

Pick an animal and symbol for your project to represent yourself:

Create a background pattern of objects based on information above found at the library or on the internet. Then cut and paste an animal symbol for yourself on top. Any media will work for this; try colored pencil, marker, or painted paper.

Student edition has a sketch page next →

Name Project Worksheet

My favorite Foods.

____

____

____

____

My hobbies or sports.

____

____

____

____

Where have I been on vacation before?

____

____

____

____

Pets I have had.

____

____

____

Favorite songs of musicians.

____

____

____

Stuff I collect.

____

____

____

____

____

My favorite holiday(s).

____

____

What I would buy if I won the lottery.

____

____

____

____

____

____

What makes me unique?

____

____

____

____

____

____

Can you use the information from this worksheet to illustrate your name in another language?

Languages that don't look like English @ Translate.google.com

Amharic
Arabic
Armenian
Assamese
Belarusian
Bengali
Bhojpuri
Chinese (either style)
Dhivehi
Dogri
Greek
Gujarati
Hebrew
Hindi
Japanese
Kannada
Kazakh
Khmer
Korean

Kurdish (Sorani)
Kyrgyz
Macedonian
Maithili
Malayalam
Marathi
Meiteilon
Mongolian
Myanmar *(Burmese)*
Nepali
Odia (Oriya)
Pashto
Persian
Punjabi
Quechua
Russian
Sanskrit
Serbian
Sindhi

Sinhala
Tajik
Tamil
Tatar
Telugu
Thai
Tigrinya
Ukrainian
Urdu
Yiddish

Eric → Chinese → 埃里克

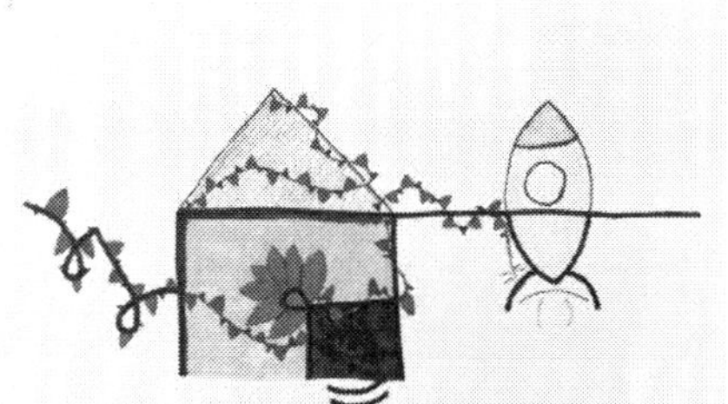

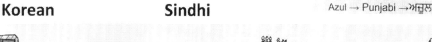

Azul → Punjabi → ਅਜ਼ੁਲ

Promise → Armenian → խոստում

Amanda 阿曼达

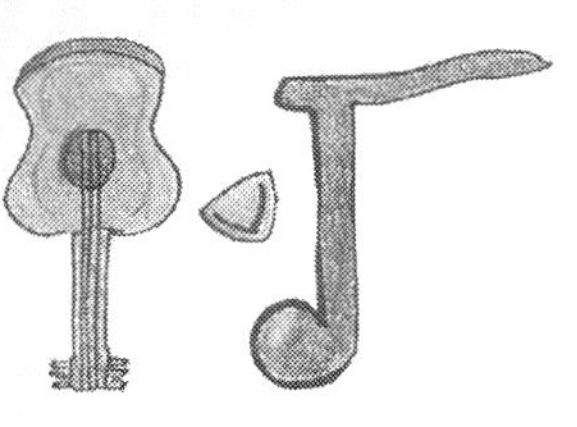

MONICA 莫尼卡

Ernie 欧内斯特

This page is not in the student edition

A Day of Dada

Dada art began about the same time as World War One (About 1916). It was a terrible war fought mostly in Europe and was thought to be the war to end all wars... but it was not. The people of Europe struggled, it was often chaotic. So awful that the Dada artists decided if the world did not make sense, their art should not make sense either! Even the name for their style was chosen by randomly placing a knife in a dictionary that happened to land on the word "Dada," a French word for 'hobbyhorse.' Marcel DuChamp was a famous Dada artist who once brought a urinal to an exhibition. He even signed it with a fake name, R. Mutt. It made people angry, they fought over it. They thought it was insulting to have a toilet in the middle of a famous gallery! Marcel laughed. You see, art is supposed to make you feel something. If the people walked into the gallery and ignored his toilet, it would have just been a toilet. But because this object, a urinal, made them angry and upset, it made them "feel" something. THEY MADE IT ART!

What are some common objects you have around you that you feel are interesting?

____

Which one could you get and turn into a work of Dada art? ___________________________

What is some strange or confusing name you can give it? Something in another language? Something spelled backwards? Maybe something random? You can even use your birthday to find a random name. Grab a book, and open to the page of your birth month, then count the words for your birthday. If you were born on Halloween, you would go to page 10 (October), and find the 31st word.

What name do you choose? ____

To finish your work of Dada art, you need to make a label to explain it and possibly confuse people even more. You should write a paragraph to go with your work of art. It does not have to make sense at all, but it has to sound important, and thoughtful. So if I had a paper clip, and named it "Vesuvius" this could be my paragraph:

Vesuvius was a great volcano that destroyed the civilization of Pompeii, a great and terrible tragedy that twisted the world in ways we could never imagine. This twisted piece of metal is deeply connected to the metals found under the ground and forced up to the surface by geomagnetic forces we still do not understand, like volcanoes. This junction of metal and twist is the perfect symbol of the Pompeii experience which we will never understand. As we touch paperclips on a daily basis and do not give them much thought, so too we ignore the people and city of Pompeii.

Resource: https://www.artedguru.com/home/a-day-of-dada

My Dada art object is ____

My title for my Dada object is: ____

____

My explanation for my art is : ____

____

____

____

____

____

____

____

____

____

____

____

____

Share your writing, and have a classmate make some suggestions here to improve or focus it:

____

____

____

NUMBERS as a Theme

Create a painting, illustration or sculpture based on a number theme.
Work as a group or individually. Research and find more
About your chosen topic, or discover a new one!

2
Good and evil
Yin and Yang
Noah's Ark, 2 of each animal
Twins

3
Holy Trinity
Ages of man
Branches of government
Strikes
Jewels of Buddhism
Pure Ones of Taoism
Hear no evil, see no evil, speak no evil

4
Seasons
Beauties of China
Elements
Archangels in Islam
Four Horsemen of the Apocalypse
The four Gospels

5
Fingers
Books of Moses and Psalms
Basic pillars of Islam
Mayan Worlds
In India, mythological headless male warriors

6
Tastes
Foods placed on the Passover Seder Plate
Articles of belief of Islam.
Degrees of Separation
Cardinal directions: N. S. E. W, up, and down

7
Deadly sins
Virtues
Wonders of the world
Continents
Seas
Colors of the rainbow
Seven days of creation
Fires of hell and doors of Hell
Asian Lucky Gods

8
Days of Hanukkah
The number of Angels carrying the Throne of Allah
"The Immortals" Chinese demigods

9
Planets
Choirs of angels

10
The Commandments
Plagues
Lost Tribes
Branches of the tree of life
Canadian provinces

11
Soccer players
Cricket players
Football Players
Incarnations of Doctor Who
Guns in a military salute

12
Apostles
Cranial nerves
Olympians
Tribes of Israel
Days of Christmas
Months

13
Baker's Dozen
Attendees of the Last Supper
Witches in a coven
Colonies of the USA

SERVICE PROJECT - Survey

The art department will create a project based on the community and recognizing its needs. Students will complete this form to help identify a specific need that should be brought to our attention. Our focus will be on intolerance within the school and community.

This could be about special needs students and students using the word "Retarded" or some group you feel is misunderstood and subjected to undue disrespect, ignorance, and intolerance.

What local social group should we focus on? Why?____

____

____

____

____

What do people not know about this group? ____

____

____

____

____

How does the intolerance hurt this group and hurt our community? ______________________________

____

____

____

____

What can be done to bring attention to this issue? ____

____

____

(The next few pages are a sample service project the author used to inform the community of bias language and bring awareness to bullying.)

TEACHER NOTE: *Service projects can take on MANY forms; this is one that was successful for us. You may wish to create your own survey for students to identify a "need" in your community and compile ideas on how to help or meet that need. One could do an auction, beautification project, donations of materials, etc.*

Design Agency

Team Name__________________________ Topic ______________________________
Members ____ Period _____

Your task is to create a poster to make people aware of the intolerance some face in school and help educate our community through posters. Posters will need to have a professional look and follow the layout of the Autism Sample. Your group will need to do some research on your chosen group so that your facts are accurate. Completed posters will be presented to the design firm CEO (teacher) for assessment.
(Sample on next page)

Posters that meet all of the requirements will be laminated and placed throughout the building and later throughout the community.

Write your ideas below and present them to your manager (teacher) for approval. Passes for research to the library can be given if necessary.

Once research and design is complete, the group will complete a sketch before beginning a final poster.

Sample Poster

AUTISM

Students with Autism are in our school and community.
Insults can be hurtful, mean and intolerant.

FACTS:

— Autism is a neurological disorder characterized by impaired social interaction and communication.

— 1 in every 150 children is diagnosed with autism.

— The cause is currently unknown but does have a genetic link.

We could learn a lot from crayons; some are sharp, some are pretty, some are dull, some have weird names, and all are different colors....but they all exist very nicely in the same box.

Poster by students of __________________________ School Art Department

SERVICE PROJECT PLAN

Team ____________________________________ Period ___________
Topic ____________________________________

What does your team already know about this topic? What are facts you think you know?

What are some common misconceptions people have about the topic you have chosen?

Who on your team will be in charge of research?

Who will be in charge of design layout?

Who will be in charge of the written portion or the poster?

Who will oversee coloring to be sure everything is neat and professional-looking?

Student edition has sketch page next

While your team member uses the pass below, please use the time to sketch a basic layout of your poster on small paper provided. This does not have to be neat, but should include all the required elements

---

Pass to __________ *to research the topic of* ___________________________________

Student: ________________________________ *Period:* _____ *From room* _____

DATE: ____/____/____ ***Signature*** ____

Service Project: *FOLLOW-UP*

Name ______________________________ Period ________

For each poster completed (up to 6) for the class, describe something you learned.

1. Poster theme: ______________________________. I learned that… ______________

____

____

2. Poster theme: ______________________________. I learned that… ______________

____

____

3. Poster theme: ______________________________. I learned that… ______________

____

____

4. Poster theme: ______________________________. I learned that… ______________

____

____

5. Poster theme: ______________________________. I learned that… ______________

____

____

6. Poster theme: ______________________________. I learned that… ______________

____

____

Where in the school was our poster placed? ______________________________________

Where in the community was our poster placed? __________________________________

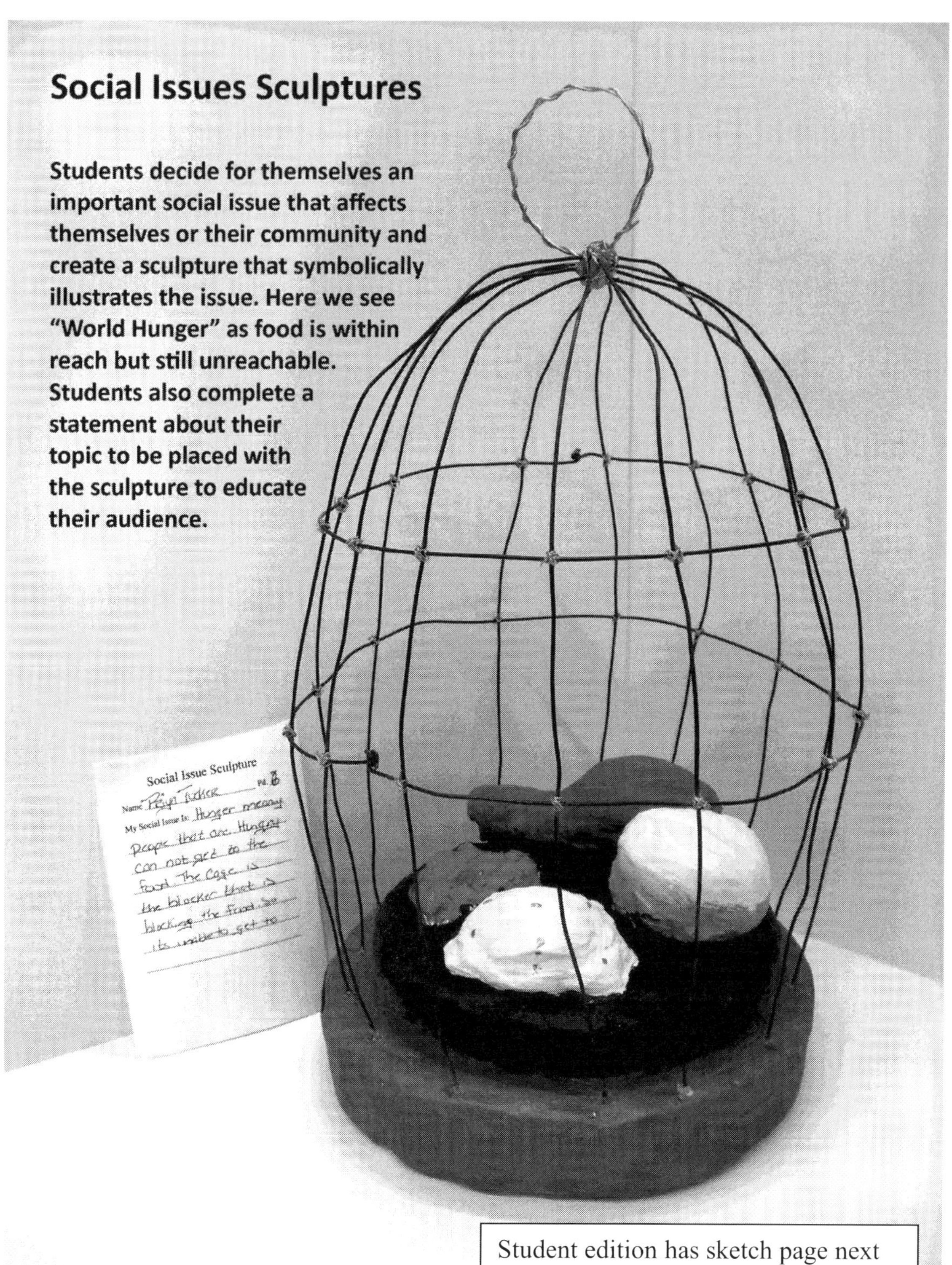

Social Issues Sculptures

Students decide for themselves an important social issue that affects themselves or their community and create a sculpture that symbolically illustrates the issue. Here we see "World Hunger" as food is within reach but still unreachable. Students also complete a statement about their topic to be placed with the sculpture to educate their audience.

Student edition has sketch page next

Social Issues

What are some social issues that affect your family, community, or school?

____________________ ____________________

____________________ ____________________

____________________ ____________________

____________________ ____________________

Which one do you think you know the most about or would like to explore more?

____

How might you symbolically represent that in a sculpture? Sketch or write below.

Sunset Silhouette

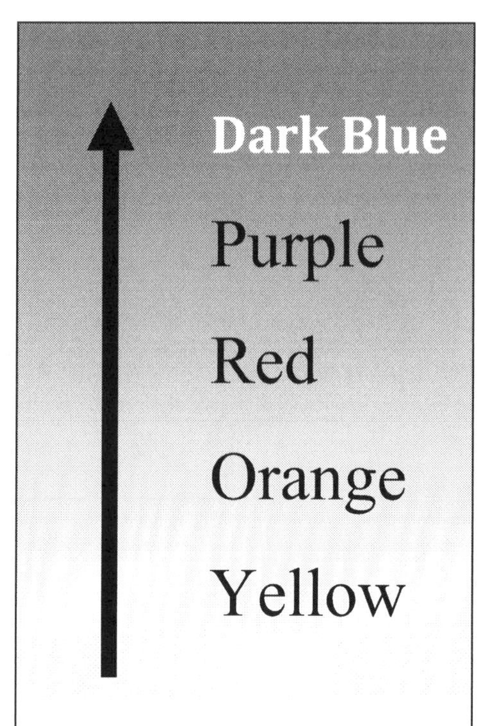

STEP 1: Starting from the bottom with YELLOW, create stripes of color that OVERLAP a little from one color to the next. (About 1 inch of overlap.)

STEP 2: Use the corner of a 6x folded piece of paper towel to blend the colors. be sure the transition from one color to the next is smooth and well blended.

Step 3: Add a horizon with a dark cool color, and fill in below it.

Step 4: Add a tree and 2 objects in black to your picture. Avoid putting things ON the horizon, they should be a bit below.

Comic Book Ideas

https://bit.ly/ComicLesson

Parody: Making fun of something, twisting what you know for a comic effect.

Superman → Stupidman
Terminator → Worminator
Godzilla → Tellitubbyzilla
Lord of The Rings → Lord of the Ring-Dings

What are a few movies you could make fun of?

________________________ → ________________________

________________________ → ________________________

________________________ → ________________________

Try changing the title of something for a funny idea…

Teenage Mutant Ninja ________
Killer _______ from Outer Space
Attack of the Mutant __________

Your idea: ____

Try a new situation…

Iron Man vs. Barney
T-Rex comes to Sesame Street
The President visits our school

Your idea: ____

There are millions of possibilities!

Do you cartoon already and have an original character???
This is a great chance to make THAT look professional.

ORIGINALITY COUNTS: Don't COPY known work.

For full credit, comic books need to include title, subtitle, dramatic action, logo, foreground, middle-ground, and background, items exiting the page, and overlap.

ME as a comic book character:

List 5 super powers you wish you had.

___: ______________________________

___: ______________________________

___: ______________________________

___: ______________________________

___: ______________________________

Go back and number them from most to least favorite.

List 3 of your unique fashion/physical features (Glasses, headband, tattoo?)

1. ______________________________
2. ______________________________
3. ______________________________

Would you be a hero or villain? ___________

Why? ______________________________

____

What might your super name be? ______________________________

What would be an amazing thing or adventure you could do as that character?

____

____

Both villains and heroes usually have side-kicks. Who/what would be your side kick?

____

What would be their lame super power? *(It can't be as good as yours 'cause they're a side kick)*

____

____

On sketch paper do a sketch of how you and your sidekick might look like. Your character may look VERY different than you, but there should be some connection to them. Be sure your character also has your 3 features. If you always wear glasses, your character might also. (You can fix/change/adjust those if you like)

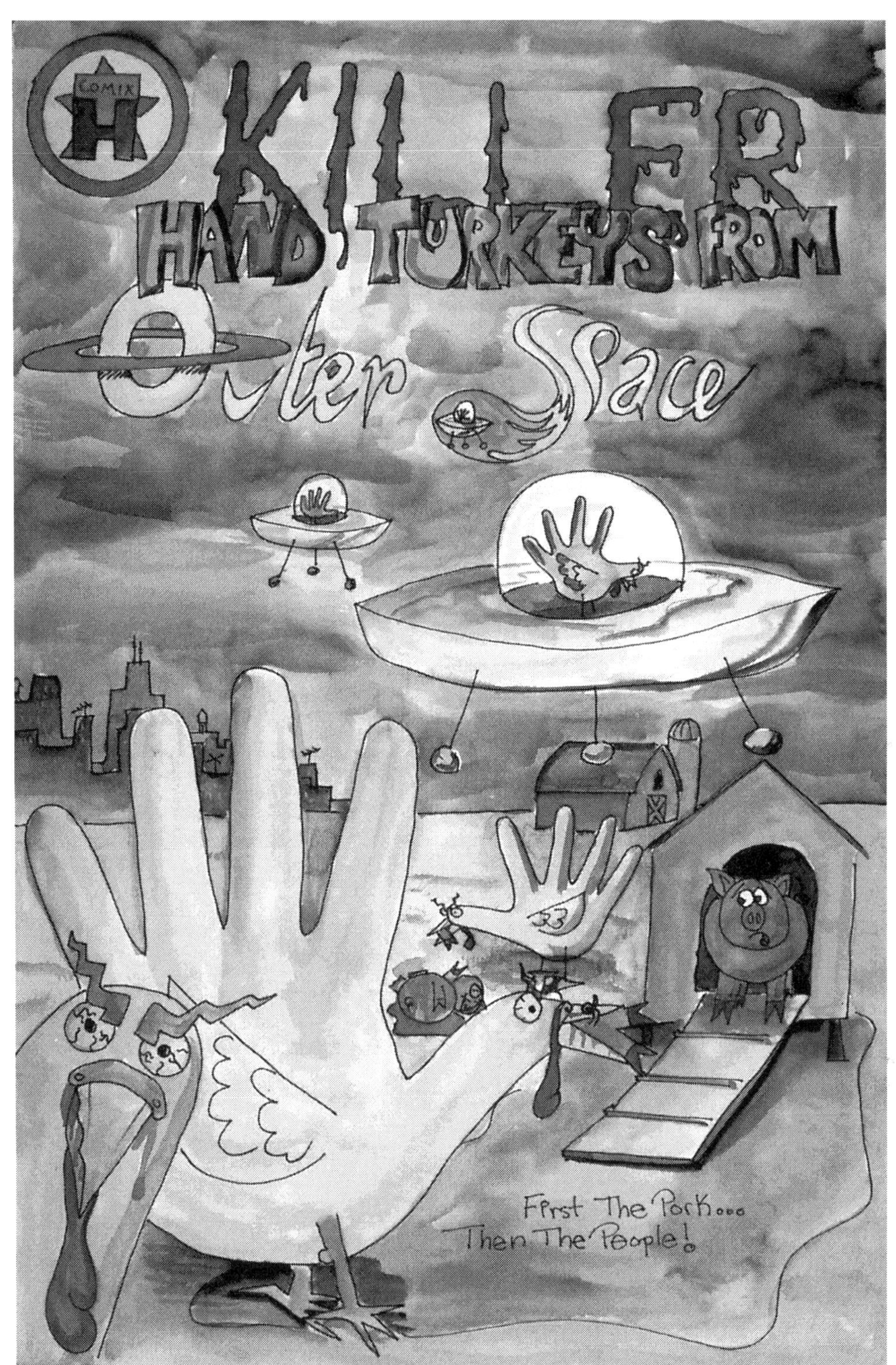

Title, subtitle, dramatic action, logo, foreground, middle-ground, background, items exiting the page, and overlap.

Student Edition has a sketch page next -->

Expressive Words

Love
Hate
Flight
Death
Burial
Crazy
Strong
Sad
Depressed
Suicidal
Hopeful
Grace
Dirty
Disgrace
Shame
Pride
Hero
Sinful
Pius
Travel
Risk
Anger
Contentment
Gluttony
Lazy
Narcissism
Turmoil
Heaven
Hell
Regal
Eternal
Complex
Simplicity

Compound Words

Horseshoe
House fly
Dragonfly
Football
Hotdog
Rainbow
Waterfall
Groundhog
Butterfly
Fireman
Firefighter
Dog food
Toenail
Jellyfish
Starfish
Catfish…
Family tree
Football…
Carpet
Honeybee
Hairnet
Hairspray
Cheese grater
French fry
French toast
Hummingbird
Pancake
Shoehorn
Boxing ring
Earring

Other?

____

Tutorial: https://youtu.be/sXqHFBHTlyw

JABBERWOCKY
Lewis Carroll
(from *Through the Looking-Glass*, 1872)

`Twas brillig, and the slithy toves
  Did gyre and gimble in the wabe;
All mimsy were the borogoves,
  And the mome raths outgrabe.

"Beware the Jabberwock, my son!
  The jaws that bite, the claws that catch!
Beware the Jubjub bird, and shun
  The frumious Bandersnatch!"

He took his vorpal sword in hand:
  Long time the manxome foe he sought --
So rested he by the Tumtum tree,
  And stood awhile in thought.

And, as in uffish thought he stood,
  The Jabberwock, with eyes of flame,
Came whiffling through the tulgey wood,
  And burbled as it came!

One, two! One, two! And through and through
  The vorpal blade went snicker-snack!
He left it dead, and with its head
  He went galumphing back.

"And, has thou slain the Jabberwock?
  Come to my arms, my beamish boy!
O frabjous day! Callooh! Callay!"
  He chortled in his joy.

`Twas brillig, and the slithy toves
  Did gyre and gimble in the wabe;
All mimsy were the borogoves,
  And the mome raths outgrabe.

Try and do a translation of each stanza, Remember, often there is no correct answer, but there is a story here…

Repeated from above, no translation needed.

Resource: https://www.artedguru.com/home/jabberwocky

Above is a painting based on the Jabberwocky, and below a pop-up version.

This page is not in the student edition

Independent Project Exploration:

If you feel students are ready to explore on their own, the following pages include a scaffold to help students explore independently yet still be held accountable for their work or lack of it. This is how my *Art Workbook for Advanced Art Students* is organized. If you wish students to tie their work of historical periods or cultures, the list below can be copied and given as a hand-out.

Inspirational Topics List

Which Historical Period/Culture/Contemporary artist will you reference in your project? Fill in blank space with the specific area, media, or artist you have chosen to explore.

[__] Gothic (1200s - 1400s)
[__] Renaissance (Italian or Northern)
[__] Baroque
[__] Rococo
[__] Neo-Classical
[__] Romanticism
[__] Realism
[__] Impressionism
[__] Fauvism
[__] Art Nouveau
[__] Art Deco
[__] Cubism
[__] Expressionism
[__] Dada
[__] Surrealism
[__] Abstract Expressionism
[__] Pop Art
[__] Op Art

[__] Asian ______________________________
[__] African ____________________________
[__] European __________________________
[__] Latin ______________________________
[__] Middle Eastern ____________________
[__] Native American __________________
[__] Aboriginal ________________________
[__] Ancient Egypt _____________________
[__] Other ______________________________
[__] Contemporary Artist ______________
[__] Contemporary Artist ______________
[__] Contemporary Artist ______________

Independent Project: Choose a School of Art, Culture, or Artist
****Student edition contains pages for 2 independent explorations. Only one sample is in this book***.*

Inspirational Topic: ______________________________ Date(s) _______________

Define it: ____

____

Name 4 famous examples:

1. ______________________________ by __________________________ Year ______

2. ______________________________ by __________________________ Year ______

3. ______________________________ by __________________________ Year ______

4. ______________________________ by __________________________ Year ______

What do all these works have in common?

____

____

____

What specific themes, ideas, impact, or techniques came from this work?

____

____

____

What could I create that might be inspired by these works, themes, ideas, or techniques?

Three Ideas:

1. ____

2. ____

3. ____

Create a thumbnail for one of these ideas on the next page.

Ideas:

Project Documentation

You will be required to attach this paper or have it available with your project. **If you lose it, points will be deducted from the project's grade.** You will be given a lot of freedom to work at your own pace, but progress must be made and recorded regularly. This paper will be evidence of your daily participation.

The inspiration for this project is ____

My concept is ____

It is connected to the inspirational idea by: ______________________________

____

Project Title:

____

Intro. date ___/___/______

Sketch complete ___/___/______

Transfer design ___/___/______

Begin final proj. ___/___/______

DEADLINE: ___/___/______

Outline steps below (pencil, pen, erase, color,...)

1. ____________________ ___/___/______

2. ____________________ ___/___/______

3. ____________________ ___/___/______

4. ____________________ ___/___/______

5. ____________________ ___/___/______

6. ____________________ ___/___/______

7. ____________________ ___/___/______

...Instructor Section Only...

10% ____________

20% ____________

25% ____________ (quarter)

30 % ____________

40% ____________

50% ____________ (half)

60% ____________

70% ____________

75% ____________ (3/4)

80% ____________

85% ____________

90% ____________

95% ____________

(Percent complete, not a grade)

Project Title ____ Date __________

Name ____ Period _________

Universal Art Project Rubric

	Criteria				Points
	100% / 20pts Exceeds Expectations	90% / 18pts Meets Expectations	80% / 16pts Approaches Expt.	70% - 65% / 14pts Missed Expt.	0/F
Elements & Principles of Design	Write how you exceeded expectations in this column	Expected use of and combination of art elements and principles that work well together for the overall design. Meeting expectations. Work demonstrates an expected use of concepts.	Acceptable use of art elements and principles but lacking harmonization or demonstration of planning or understanding.	Lacks evidence of thoughtful use of elements and principles with a design that looks unplanned, rushed, and/or incomplete.	___
Craftsmanship Neatness		Overall, the project is clean and without major defects like Folds/Rips. All areas have been considered and finished to meet expectations.	Minor folds or stray marks may be present but the work is acceptable. Some portions of the work could have benefited by more attention to detail.	Work includes obvious deficits like folds, rips, and/or stray marks. Little effort went into creating the work and using information demonstrated.	___
Time & Management		Student was mostly independently motivated with a few social distractions. Work was mostly self-driven.	Student was somewhat distracted from their work and had to be reminded to stay on-task. More focus would have been helpful.	Often reminded to stay on task. Social/digital interactions impeded work. Lack of focus had a strong impact on project work.	___
Execution, Originality, & Uniqueness		Work was unique & original with some evidence from samples/examples. Work included no direct copying from other sources.	Though work did include some sample or derivative imagery, it did include many unique elements.	What work was done was highly derivative of the samples or other student's work. Little was truly original or unique.	___
Requirements & Depth		Subject and media were well explored and met project expectations.	Subject or technique was not fully explored. A requirement was missing.	Little depth of subject and technique. Requirements were not fully met.	___
Comments:				**Grade**	___

Teacher Resource: https://www.artedguru.com/home/monday-art-quotes

Video Introduction: https://youtu.be/W5PrQiJVWW8

A: Please take 2 or 3 minutes to write about the following quote.

What is meant by the following quote?

"I'm not an abstractionist. I'm not interested in the relationship of color or form or anything else. I'm interested only in expressing basic human emotions: tragedy, ecstasy, doom, and so on." ~ Mark Rothko Video: http://y2u.be/E1lcO9ncz90

____

____

____

B: Please take 2 or 3 minutes to write about the following quote.

What is meant by the following quote?

Your ego can become an obstacle to your work. If you start believing in your greatness, it is the death of your creativity. ~ Marina Abramovic Video: http://y2u.be/IhbiVceuR0o

____

____

____

C: Please take 2 or 3 minutes to write about the following quote.

What is meant by the following quote?

In speaking of his time as a child in a mental institution, "They took the clay away – child abuse" ~Alonzo Clemons, *"Savant, Sculptor and Artist" 05/10/19* **http://y2u.be/RrW4upZoXHA**

____

____

____

D: Please take 2 or 3 minutes to write about the following quote.

What is meant by the following quote?

"I make my art in silence. The materials conjure ideas. The ideas conjure images. The images conjure art. The art conjures feelings. The feelings are the goal." ~Betye Saar

Video: http://y2u.be/T7CFz9xzhIM

____

____

____

E: Please take 2 or 3 minutes to write about the following quote.

What is meant by the following quote?

"I realized at a young age that art was there for me to create conversation and a relationship with people. It allowed me to become approachable to my peers, who might not have otherwise understood me." ~ Alana Tillman Video: http://y2u.be/W0FEY6JWdUE

____

____

____

F: Please take 2 or 3 minutes to write about the following quote.

What is meant by the following quote?

Art builds empathy and an understanding of other humans that will lead us to see ourselves in one another, and thus grow a family rather than a society. This is about how beautiful we are when we get to see all of us. ~ Roberto Lugo Video http://y2u.be/NH02Hrj60B0

____

____

____

G: Please take 2 or 3 minutes to write about the following quote.

What is meant by the following quote?

For me, art can reflect the celebration of the simple and good things in life. This is most important to me! ~Romero Britto Video: http://y2u.be/nZFIHI0MOnY

____

____

____

H: Please take 2 or 3 minutes to write about the following quote.

What is meant by the following quote?

"Every idea occurs while you are working. If you are sitting around waiting for inspiration, you could sit there forever." ~ Chuck Close Video: http://y2u.be/tXsuo4NWOUY

____

____

____

I: Please take 2 or 3 minutes to write about the following quote.

What is meant by the following quote?

"A true artist is not one who is inspired, but one who inspires others. What is important is to spread confusion, not eliminate it." ~Salvador Dali'
Video: https://vimeo.com/145418153

____

____

____

J: Please take 2 or 3 minutes to write about the following quote.

What is meant by the following quote?

"We don't make mistakes. We just have happy accidents." ~Bob Ross

Video: http://y2u.be/OX-kO2eomoI

____

____

____

K: Please take 2 or 3 minutes to write about the following quote.

What is meant by the following quote?

In reflecting on spending 45 year in prison for a crime he didn't commit: "I didn't actually think I'd ever be free again. This art is what I did to stay sane," ~Richard Phillips

Video: http://y2u.be/aWKZ9P1N-n0

____

____

____

L: Please take 2 or 3 minutes to write about the following quote.

What is meant by the following quote?

"There are many accidents that are nothing but accidents-and forget it. But there are some that were brought about only because you are the person you are... you have the wherewithal, intelligence, and energy to recognize it and do something with it."

~Helen Frankenthaler **Video: http://y2u.be/7efK8UTjlzY**

____

____

____

M: Please take 2 or 3 minutes to write about the following quote.

What is meant by the following quote?

"Red is one of the strongest colors, it's blood, it has a power with the eye. That's why traffic lights are red I guess, and stop signs as well... In fact I use red in all of my paintings." ~Keith Haring Video: http://y2u.be/8eE4Dm8EGTg

____

____

____

N: Please take 2 or 3 minutes to write about the following quote.

What is meant by the following quote?

What's important about the artists we learn about in art history and see in all the art books is that they have somehow pushed the boundaries of what people think art is or should be, and that's how they've made their work relevant. That's what I'm trying to figure out for myself. ~Kadir Nelson Video: http://y2u.be/01yRoSrhQME

____

____

____

O: Please take 2 or 3 minutes to write about the following quote.

What is meant by the following quote?

"Art should comfort the disturbed and disturb the comfortable." ~ Banksy

Video: http://y2u.be/MMoVoWXBorg

____

____

____

P: Please take 2 or 3 minutes to write about the following quote.

After watching this video, what is meant by the following quote? http://y2u.be/cZ-j4UbyKCU

"My paintings represent my happy personality. I always want to do beautiful paintings." ~Ellen Kane

____

____

____

Q: Please take 2 or 3 minutes to write about the following quote.

What is meant by the following quote?

"The idea is to make visible those who are practically invisible in the city, humanize public spaces." - VHILS (Alexandre Farto) Video: http://y2u.be/P8_nZTVaaNw

____

____

____

R: Please take 2 or 3 minutes to write about the following quote.

What is meant by the following quote?

"All of depiction is fiction, it's only a question of degree." ~Titus Kaphar

Video: http://y2u.be/_GmoWXl1uOA

____

____

____

S: Please take 2 or 3 minutes to write about the following quote.

What is meant by the following quote?

"What I am seeking is not the real and not the unreal but rather the unconscious, the mystery of the instinctive in the human race." ~Amedeo Modigliani

Video: http://y2u.be/8541kuU0I8M

____

____

____

T: Please take 2 or 3 minutes to write about the following quote.

What is meant by the following quote?

"Painting is a poem and a poem is a painting." ~Tyrus Wong http://y2u.be/fxFAQZdnXQU

____

____

____

U: Please take 2 or 3 minutes to write about the following quote.

What is meant by the following quote?

"I put the viewer to work, to keep them imagining." ~Shirley Woodson

Video: http://y2u.be/bKb4edvsxss

____

____

____

V: Please take 2 or 3 minutes to write about the following quote.

What is meant by the following quote?

"I honestly believed everybody in the world wanted to make abstract paintings, and people only became lawyers and doctors and brokers and things because they couldn't make abstract paintings." ~Frank Stella Video: http://y2u.be/G3rxnr8tUYA

____

____

____

W: Please take 2 or 3 minutes to write about the following quote.

What is meant by the following quote?

"I'm a musician trapped in the body of a glass artist" ~Preston Singletary

Video: http://y2u.be/URItBWc5zXQ

____

____

____

X: Please take 2 or 3 minutes to write about the following quote.

What is meant by the following quote?

"I don't think you can create art out of anger; it has to come out of some form of understanding. You have to feel good about who you are and that you could do something to change things." ~Faith Ringgold Video: http://y2u.be/IZ-VvOep2D8

____

____

____

Y: Please take 2 or 3 minutes to write about the following quote.

What is meant by the following quote?

"To be an artist at twenty is to be twenty: to still be an artist at fifty is to be an artist."

~E. Gibbons as inspired by Eugene Delacroix's quote about poets.

Video: http://y2u.be/V0TdVj2kCoU

Z: Please take 2 or 3 minutes to write about the following quote.

What is meant by the following quote?

"Painting is like a sort of sickness, I think." ~Joan Mitchell

Video: http://y2u.be/XQ0pbQf1Nqo

1: Write your own quote about art.

Art Principles of Design Sample

"Day and Night" by M.C. Escher

UNITY: Same-ness throughout an image:
The whole image is in black and white unifying the picture through limited color.

VARIETY: (Contrast): Differences throughout an image
The images have a variety of different things like birds, towns, rivers, and fields.

EMPHASIS: How one thing stands out above all others in some way.
The white bird to the right stands out because it is so bright against the dark background.

MOVEMENT: Might be real or suggested movement..
The birds appear to be flying in opposite directions, giving a sense of movement.

BALANCE: (Symmetrical vs Asymmetrical Balance, Predictable or non-predictable balance)
The image above is symmetrically balanced because the left is a mirror image of the right.
Even distribution of "visual weight."

PATTERN: (Shapes, forms, lines…) Repeated motifs that create a predictable or unpredictable pattern.
The birds create an alternating regular pattern in both their positive and negative space.
OR: The fields in the background make a regular pattern like a quilt.

CONTRAST: Opposites. They can be visual or suggested by mood or subject too.
The white birds on the right are in contrast to the blue birds on the left.
OR: The birds in the foreground appear much larger than the buildings in the background.

Emotional Values of Shapes and Colors

There are some symbols in cultures that are the same everywhere. For instance, a puddle of red will be assumed to be blood; this would be the same in New York, China, or the jungles of some far off land.

Artists have been using these cultural symbols in their art to hide the meanings of their work or to code them. Here is a simple list. Remember shapes and colors can be combined for mixed emotional values. A heart shape is a combination of circles and a triangle.

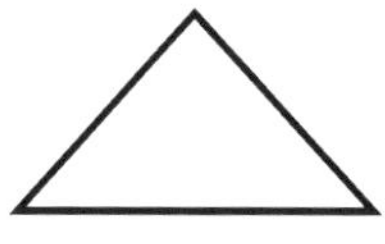

Triangles are associated with *SHARP* objects like a knife, a sword, broken glass, and spear. They are considered aggressive, dangerous, negative, and unbalanced. Triangles can be drawn in many ways to make them look more or less sharp.

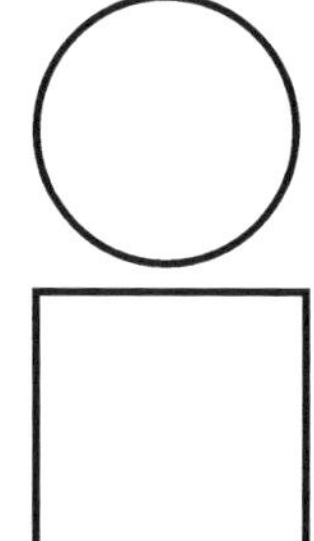

Circles are associated with SOFT objects like a balloon, bubble, or ball. They are considered playful, soft, energetic, positive, and happy.

Squares are associated with constructive ideas like building. They are regular, stable, strong, dependable, and at times, monotonous. Stretching the square into a rectangle can break up the monotony.

Red: Associated with blood, aggression, anger

Orange: Aggressive but not deadly. (Like Tackle Football)

Gold: A color of richness and wealth. Also a color of accomplishment. (Like a Gold Award)

Yellow: Playful, warm, enthusiastic, giddy, and child-like

Green: A color of growth. The type of green can indicate freshness

Blue: Associated with the sky or water, it is vast, cool, quenching, life-giving, and generally positive

Purple: A deep dark sky, royalty, peaceful, calm, and quiet

Black: A color of mystery or the unknown, also a color of heaviness and matter

Brown: Earth, soil, dirt. A color of potential growth, possibilities, a new beginning, or the end

White: A color of light, spirituality, and purity

MIXING colors will give new meanings and associations, so will using colored patterns.

Color Vocabulary

This vocabulary may be on an exam, along with your 8 Art Element Information and Art Principles of Design.

Value The intensity of a color, its saturation as compared to another color. "Pink has a lighter value than red, but a darker value than white."

Shading Changing the value by adding black or white.

Chiaroscuro Italian word for light and dark. It is the change in the highlights and shadows.

Spectrum White light separated into its primary and secondary colors. They are in order: red, orange, yellow, green, blue and purple.

Hue Is the actual color without shade or highlight.

Primary Colors The 3 colors that mix to make every other color. (red, blue, yellow)

Secondary Colors The first mixes of the primary colors. (orange, green, purple) KNOW how to make each secondary color!!!

Intermediate Colors These are the colors between the primary and secondary colors, sometimes called tertiary (Ter-She-Airy) colors.

Complementary Colors Colors on the opposite sides of the color wheel, considered direct opposites like red and green.

Analogous Colors Neighboring colors on the color wheel, like yellow and orange, or blue and green.

Monochromatic Colors Different values of the same hue or color. Changing one color from light to dark. A black and white photo is monochromatic or one all in blues…

Intensity The brightness or dullness of a color.

Color Harmonies Colors that are grouped together for effect. Generally analogous colors are considered harmonious or varying versions of a single color. (see monochromatic).

Warm Colors Colors that are more energetic and seem to come forward. When you think of fire, you'll know these colors are red, yellow and orange.

Cool Colors Colors that are less energetic and seem to recede. When you think of water, you may recall that these colors are blue, green and purple.

Elements Assessment

1
2
3
4
balance
black
brown
circle
color
cone
cool
cube
cylinder
dark
depth
element
form
length
light
line
mass
negative
neutral
point
positive
primary
rectangle
reflected
secondary
shadow
shape
space
sphere
square
texture
triangle
warm
white
width

All possible answers are in the list on the left. Some answers are repeated, some are never used. Crossing off answers may not be helpful. The "#" sign means the answer is a number.

A line is a ________ moving through ________. We can measure the _______ of a line and nothing else, therefore it is _#_______ dimensional or _#_______ -D.

A ________ that intersects itself will create a shape. A shape is _#_______ dimensional. There are _#_______ basic shapes. The one with the fewest amount of sides is the __________, and the one with the most sides is the _________.

A ________ that moves in _________ can create a form. There are _#_______ basic forms. The one with the fewest amount of sides is the __________. The one with the most sides is the _________.

There are _#_______ basic colors. Basic colors are also called _______ colors. When these basic colors mix they create ________ colors of which there are _#________. Color is _______ light. Orange, Red and Yellow are considered _________ colors, while Blue, Green and Purple are considered ________ colors.

_________ refers to the weight of something; sometimes it is real and sometimes it is the way it looks. A _________ colored box will look heavier than a _________ colored one.

The roughness or smoothness of a surface refers to its __________. It can sometimes be made by repeating an art ___________ many times.

All objects, art and non-art, take up ________. Many art elements move through it. This art element comes in 2 types, they are _____________ meaning where the object IS, and ____________, meaning where the object is NOT.

The art element of ________ helps us see all other art elements. We see everything because it is ___________ off of an object or surface and back to our eye. When it is NOT bounced back to us we see __________.

8 Art Elements Review

USE this information **WITH** Art Principles! Principles **organize** the Elements!
A **line** is a point moving through space. We can measure the length of a line and nothing else about it; therefore it is one-dimensional or 1-D.

A line that intersects itself will create a **shape**. A shape is 2-dimensional. There are 3 basic shapes. They are the triangle, circle, and square.

A shape that moves in space can create a **form**. There are 4 basic forms. They are the cylinder, cone, cube, and sphere.

There are 3 basic **colors**. Basic colors are also called primary colors. When these basic colors mix they create secondary colors of which there are 3. Color is reflected light. Orange, red, and yellow are considered warm colors, while blue, green, and purple are considered cool colors. KNOW color wheel and mixtures!!!! Complementary = opposite, analogous = neighboring.

Mass refers to the weight of something, sometimes it is real and sometimes it is the way it looks. A dark colored box will look heavier than a light colored one.*

The roughness or smoothness of a surface refers to its **texture**. It can sometimes be made by repeating an art element many times. For example if you draw 100 lines, they will no longer be seen as lines, but as a texture; like grass.

All objects, art and non-art, take up **space**. Many art elements move through it. This art element comes in 2 types; Positive Space, meaning where the object IS, and Negative Space, meaning where the object is NOT.

The art element of **light** helps us see all other art elements. We see everything because it is reflected off an object or surface and back to our eyes. When it is NOT bounced back to us, we see black, or nothing.*

***Mass** and **Light** are sometimes combined and called **VALUE**. When discussing 3D art Mass and light are important to separate, while 2D art often combines these elements. It is how artists create the illusion of an object looking like it is 3D when really it is on a flat surface. It is done through shading and highlighting with many techniques.

Principles of Design

What is **Contrast**? Juxtaposition. To put opposites in the same image to make each stand out. Opposites colors like red and green, or opposite shapes like circular and sharp shapes, areas of light and dark.

What is the opposite of contrast? Unity or harmony. Remember that any art element can be contrasted, just find its opposite. There are 8 art elements like line, shape, color, form, light, texture, mass, and space.

What is **Unity**? Having similarity in some way through an art element or material or theme. Like everything being red, or all parts made from squares…

What is the opposite of Unity? Contrast.

What does **Balance** Mean? Having an equal amount of stuff or visual weight in an artwork.

Symmetrical Balance = Perfect Balance.

Asymmetrical Balance = Unequal stuff, but still in balance, (A brick /giant bag of feathers)

What is **Emphasis**? A highlight of a particular area or thing.

Should the focal point be centered in an artwork? Not usually, but it can. A ***little*** off center is often true.

Where should it go? Anywhere but the center. As a general rule, putting something in the center of a painting makes it feel less like movement, like a portrait. Moving it to the side, a bit, makes it seem that it has a bit more visual energy.

What is **Variety**? Having a diverse mixture of any art element, like shape or color to avoid monotony or boredom in a work of art. A painting that includes many colors, not just one or two.

What does **Movement** Mean? Having a sense of direction, sometimes actual movement (like in a mobile) In a cartoon it can be shown with "swish lines", in a painting it may be in a blur, or an area where there is gradual or rapid change or repetition. Blur in a photograph indicates movement.

Does a sculpture have to actually move to have "Movement?" NO, it only needs to look like it could move.

What is **Pattern**? A repeated art element can create a pattern, like a repeated shape on a quilt, fabric, even leaves on a tree can be a pattern, though we would call that an organic (unpredictable) pattern.

What kind of artists use pattern? (Architects: brick pattern in a wall. Quilter…)

What 2 kinds of pattern are possible? Predictable (mechanical) and unpredictable (organic).

What is **Rhythm**? Repeated elements making a visual rhythm.

It organizes space through <u>repetition</u>. This repetition can be predictable, complicated or unpredictable.

Does it have to be regular (predictable)? No, When unpredictable, we call that "organic" or of nature.

Please Note: Color mixtures, complimentary colors, analogous colors, triads, what colors mix well, which ones do not, primary colors, and secondary colors.

Schools of Art - History

A "School Of Art" is another way to say a group of art or a style of art. We put things in groups all the time. We can put people in groups too like girls and boys. Religions are kinds of groups like Christians, Muslims, Jews, and Buddhists… Even your pets are put in groups like poodles, bull dogs, spaniels, and beagles…

We group these things by the way they look. Poodles all have curly hair, Dalmatians have black spots, Beagles are smaller and have brown spots.

Art is the same way. If you see a painting, with people wearing rich clothes like from a Cinderella Movie, and the trees look very fluffy, and the people look like they are rich and playing around, then it might be from the Rococo (Row-co-co) school of art.

If you see a painting of something you might see in a TV commercial, and it has very bright colors, it might be from the Pop Art school of art.

Rococo and Pop Art are schools of art. We will learn about 13 important ones. You should know there are hundreds of schools of art, but you will learn about just a few important ones. They are:

Renaissance (Re-na-sance)
Baroque (Ba-roke)
Rococo (Row-co-co)
Neo-Classical (Neo-Clas-si-kul)
Romanticism (Ro-man-ti-si-zum)
Realism (real-is-um)
Impressionism (Imm-pre-shon-is-um)
Cubism (Qb-is-um) or (Cube-is-um)
Dada (Da-da)
Surrealism (Sur-real-is-um)
Expressionism (X-pre-shun-is-um)
Abstract Expressionism (Ab-stract, X-pre-shun-is-um)
Pop Art

Tutorials: https://bit.ly/SchoolsOfArt

Research:

Pick one school of art from the previous page. Maybe your teacher will have you pick from a hat, so not everyone does the same thing. Write it here:

____

Use the internet or the library to answer these questions:

1. What is the year that your school of art began? ______________*
(* this may not be exact, but get as close as you can)

2. Name three artists of your school of art and their birth year

____________________________________ born in __________

____________________________________ born in __________

____________________________________ born in __________

3. Many artists start after they are 20 years old. If you add 20 to their birth year, is your answer to number 1 still correct? Do you need to change it?

4. Name three famous artworks (painting, drawing, or sculpture) and the artist.

____________________________________ made by ______________

____________________________________ made by ______________

____________________________________ made by ______________

5. What must art from your school of art need to look like to be from that style?

____

____

____

____

POSTERS:

Working with a small group of two to four people, you are to create a poster that will teach others about that school of art.

Who is in your group? (Put your name in too)

________________________________,

________________________________,

________________________________,

________________________________,

RULES: You must include:

— Title (That's the school of art)
— General dates of the school of art
— ART from that period IN COLOR (You may photocopy and color in)
— Label all artwork

Written information should include:

— Written history of that school of art
— 4 or more artists working in that period
— Each artist must be shown with an artwork on the poster
— CLUES: If you saw a painting, how would you know it was from your "School Of Art" List some clues to know how to know the art's school

Do a bit more like…

— Include an interesting fact like –Van Gogh went crazy because he held his brushes in his mouth and got slowly poisoned by his paint!
— QUOTE: Include a famous quote from artist in your school of art.

There is a sample poster on the next page and a sketch page after that.

Rococo
François Boucher lived from 1703 to 1770. He designed paintings and tapestries for the French royalty. Know for his fashionably frivolous depictions of rosy-cheeked aristocratic ladies, pudgy putti, and idealized mythological subjects. The paintings often reflected the desires of the upper classes. His idyllic representations of imaginary settings reveal contemporary cravings for escapist fantasies. Boucher demonstrated a stylistic change, and was the first to abandon the ideals of symmetry. Asymmetry became a standard for the Rococo style.
Posted here is his painting, "The Swing." Jean studied under Boucher. He produced landscapes of the Italian countryside. After painting "The Swing," there was a demand for more of his erotic pieces. With his ability to paint playful figures, he became the leader of the Rococo style. Fragonard was known for flirting with the edge of decency in his paintings.
The Swing
Jean-Honore Fragonard
Rococo began when society abandoned the formality of the earlier years and began pursuing personal amusement and happiness. Rococo is derived from the french word "rocaille" which means rock and shell garden ornamentation. Rococo included interior design, painting, architecture, and sculpture. It became fashionable in Europe, mostly in France. Rococo started in the 17th century, during the rise of the French middle class. The composition of a rococo painting was often asymmetrical. It also appealed to the senses, because it stressed beauty over depth.
Pastoral
Francois Boucher
Reunion en plein air
(Meeting in the open air)
Antoine Watteau
Jean-Baptiste Pigalle lived from 1714-1785. He studied at the French Academy, for French sculpture. He had knowledge of the Belvedere Torso or a composition by Jordeans, which is demonstrated in the freedom in Mercury's turning movement. He worked with a true understanding of anatomy and with a light, subtle sense of movement. His works demonstrate a wide range of skills. From small works appealing to the taste, to large elaborate tombs.
Mercury Attaching His Wings
Jean-Baptiste Pigalle
Antoine Watteau was of on the first Rococo artists. His paintings hand an idyllic and charming approach. He painted charming and graceful paintings showing his intrest in theatre and ballet.

Schools of Art Poster Project Sample by Students

Poster planning sketch page. School of art: ___________________________

Video Help: https://bit.ly/ResearchSupportVideo

Additional resource: https://youtu.be/9qA_aoTxL5w

Some Dead Artists

This is not to be considered a complete list of possible artists.

Pablo Picasso
Marcel Duchamp
Henri Matisse
Vincent Van Gogh
Claude Monet
Édouard Manet
Georgia O'Keeffe
Piet Mondrian
Paul Klee
Roy Lichtenstein
Elizabeth Catlett
Michelangelo
Salvador Dali
Jackson Pollack
Edmonia Lewis
Mark Rothko
Paul Cezanne
Andy Warhol
Ansel Adams
Georges Seurat
Robert Rauschenberg
Albers Joseph
Albrecht Dürer
Paul Gauguin
Louise Bourgeois
Francisco Goya
Jean-Michel Basquiat
Robert Indiana
Berthe Morisot
Joan Miró
Gustave Courbet

Grant Wood
Andrew Wyeth
Pierre Renoir
M. C. Escher
Mary Cassatt
Alexander Calder
Rembrandt Van Rijn
George Rodrigue
Dorothea Lang
Edvard Munch
Laura Knight
Duane Hanson
Louise Nevelson
Agnes Martin
Frida Kahlo
Katsushika Hokusai
Edward Hopper
Jacob Lawrence
Rosa Bonheur
Henri Rousseau
Marc Chagall
Augustus Rodin
Tamara de Lempicka
Norman Rockwell
George Segal
Grandma Moses
Elaine de Kooning
Willem de Kooning
Jacques-Louis David
Bob Ross
Dorothea Tanning

The Scenario!

The dead have come to life again! You'd think the government would be on high alert, schools would be closed, and there would be chaos everywhere... but no. Unlike pop-culture zombie movies, these dead folks are just as normal as they ever were. Most zombies have happily found jobs at McDonald's and Walmart.

Your art teacher, apparently a zombie sympathizer, has decided that this is the perfect opportunity for you to actually go out and meet a famous artist and interview them instead of writing a boring research paper.

The next few pages offer you 50 potential questions to ask, ***TOO MANY***, but your goal is to ask enough to fill out _____ full pages of interview. You can always do more but don't do less.

Other Artists: ____

Please set up your document like this:

- One inch margins on all sides, SINGLE spaced.
- 12 point, simple font like Arial, Calibri, or Times New Roman.
- Cover page with your first and last name, period, and the interview title.
- Each question and answer should not have a blank space between them.
- New questions can have one space above them.
- Include an example of the artist's work on the last page and label it.
- Bibliography on the last page under the photo. (Every web address you got info from.)

Plagiarism & the use of A.I will result in a zero. Don't do it.

Please start your interview with an introduction; it's the polite thing to do. (And required) Something like this would be okay, but please give it your own twist.
I am pleased to present to you this interview with ________ who was born ______ and sadly died on _______. They worked in a style of art called _______ in the country of ________.

Pro Tip: Backwards Design Your Interview! In the gameshow Jeopardy, they give the players an answer, and they have to say the question. You can do the same thing, just write the answers as if it was a conversation.

From Wikipedia we read: *Born into an upper-middle-class family, Van Gogh drew as a child and was serious, quiet and thoughtful, but showed signs of mental instability. As a young man, he worked as an art dealer, often travelling, but became depressed after he was transferred to London. He turned to religion and spent time as a missionary in southern Belgium. Later he drifted into ill-health and solitude. He was keenly aware of modernist trends in art and, while back with his parents, took up painting in 1881. His younger brother, Theo, supported him financially, and the two of them maintained a long correspondence.*

What are some questions this text answers?

Q: ____

____

Q: ____

____

Possible Questions:

Answer questions in a paragraph form. Simple one-word or short answers are not acceptable! If an answer is shorter than a question, DON'T USE IT! Write as if it was a conversation, be creative and have fun, *but your facts must be true.*

<u>IMPORTANT:</u> *It is perfectly acceptable to expand on a fact and make it feel more "real" like in an interview, as long as it is based on real information. So in the example from Van Gogh, we know that his younger brother supported him financially. How do you think it feels for an older brother to depend on his younger brother for financial support? Answer the question with the fact, and then expand on it to make your interview feel more real and interesting like this:*

Q: Were you able to make a living doing your art?
V.G.: I actually had to depend on my little brother for financial support I am embarrassed to say. As an elder brother, I should be the one to carry on the family name and success. My little brother should look up to me for advice and help when necessary. To know that I only sold one work of art while I was alive, and I sold it to my brother is sad. No wonder I was depressed! It got so bad I had to be institutionalized.

The first 5 questions and the <u>LAST</u> are MANDATORY:

1. **Can you tell me a bit about your family and childhood?**
2. **What kinds of art do you like to create?**
3. **What do you think makes your work unique or special?**
4. **What is your most famous work of art?** *(Describe it, include a print-out at the end of the interview and label it with title, artist's name, material, size, and year.)*
5. **What was going on in the world when you were an artist?** *(Add 20 years to their birth year and find important historical event(s) they might have known about.)*
6. How did you die?
7. What other artists or styles influenced your work?
8. What did the people of YOUR TIME think of your work?
9. Does your art have a message or political point of view?
10. Did anything unusual happen to you as a kid?
11. Were you a religious person?
12. Did religion influence your work?
13. Did you always want to be an artist?
14. Who was your favorite artist or artists?
15. Did you have any friends who were artists too?
16. Did you do any other jobs besides being an artist?
17. Do you have any regrets?
18. Were you famous and successful in life?

19. Did you have a family of your own and were they supportive?
20. Were you ever in love? (Who?)
21. Did love or the lack of love influence your work?
22. How did people come to learn about you or your work?
23. Did you participate in any important exhibitions?
24. What museums have your work?
25. How much did your work sell for during your lifetime?
26. How much might some of your artwork sell for today?
27. How did you learn to be an artist?
28. Did you learn to make art on your own or go to school for it?
29. What is something interesting about yourself not related to your art?
30. What kind of student were you in school?
31. When did you first show signs of creativity?
32. What themes or ideas inspire your creativity?
33. Though you are known for your _____, what other kind of art did you do?
34. Did you have any influential teachers, mentors, or supporters?
35. Did you fit in with your friends and neighbors or were you an outcast?
36. How old were you when you started to become well known?
37. What do people say about your art today? (Look up critical reviews)
38. Is there a work of art you made that you do not like?
39. Did you have any pets?
40. Was there a work of art by another artist that influenced you?
41. Did you ever copy another work of art and do it in your own style?
42. Are there any artists that have stolen your art by remaking it in their style?
43. What was something really good that happened in your life?
44. What kinds of problems did you experience in your life?
45. What was something really bad that happened in your life?
46. Was there something in your life you had to overcome? (...and did you?)
47. If you could change something about your life, what would it be and why?
48. If you were living and working today as an artist, would it be easier or harder? (Why?)
49. What do you hope people learn from your art?
50. What do you want people to remember most about you?

LAST Mandatory Question: What words of wisdom would you like to end this interview with? (Include a real quote by artist. If you find none, include a quote by a museum about their work.)

Please grade your own project with the rubric below before you hand it in.

	100 Exceeds Expectations	90 Meets all requirements	80 Meets most requirements	70 Meets some requirements	60 Meets few requirements	Zero Little or no evidence
Completeness	Work went beyond expectations with significant additional length, info, materials, etc.	Work was the correct length and all required elements are met.	Work was about 10% shorter than required and/or a required element was missing.	Work was about 20 to 30% shorter than required and/or a few required elements were missing.	Work was more than 25% shorter than required and/or many required elements were missing.	Hardly anything was completed. Less than 25% of required work was done.
Formatting* • **Margins/Fonts** • **cover page** • **introduction** • **labeled image** • **required length** • **websites cited** • **directions followed**	All requirements were met and some exceeded with exceptional craftsmanship and creative touches.	All requirements were met. *(See list)	One required formatting element was missing or significantly deficient; like using a larger font, or wide spacing.	Two required formatting elements were missing or deficient like the use large fonts or wide spacing or margins to hide lack of content.	More than 2 required elements missing or significantly deficient. Little evidence formatting was thoughtful.	Most or all required elements missing or significantly deficient.
Originality	Unique, significantly artful, and/or an unexpected approach to the project that enhanced its overall presentation.	The project was original without derivative elements or work copied from others.	The work was fairly original with little that was copied or borrowed from the internet or other sources. All copied info was cited.	Some portions of the work appear to be copied from other sources but cited in the bibliography.	Portions of the work appear to be copied from other sources and not cited properly, but are not willful plagiarism, just carelessness.	Little appears to be the student's original work, and/or it includes significant plagiarism.
Depth of content	All portions of the work are focused, rich, and informative. Even creative elements add to its educational value.	The work was focused and on point. None was distracting or "filler." It provided good and insightful information about the artist.	Most of the work was focused and on point. Little was distracting or "filler." It provided some good information about the artist.	Some of the work was focused and on point. Some was distracting or "filler." It provided some information about the artist.	Little of the work was focused. Much of it seemed off topic or did not provide focused information about the artist and their work.	Off topic, incoherent, providing little or no meaningful content.
Grammar Spelling Organization Proofreading	Good editing & proofreading is obvious. No errors found. Work flows beautifully; it is well organized, and thoughtful. Professional feel.	Work is free of major spelling and grammar issues. The organization of thoughts is good and free of distractions.	Work could have been improved by proofreading and some errors could have been corrected. There are a few minor organizational issues.	Work contains many issues that could have been solved by some proofreading. The flow of ideas or organization is somewhat distracting.	Grammar and spelling contain significant issues. Little attempt at proofreading is evident making this project very difficult to read.	No attempt was made to proofread or organize content at all. Careless and unfocused.

Recorded Grade ___________ Comments: ________________________________

Art History "Story Time" Assignment.

Find 4-6 famous works of art that you feel "tell a story." You will use those images as illustrations for a story you will write. When complete, you will have 2 full pages of text (if all the images were removed). There will be an additional fact sheet to include which will bring the total writing requirement to 3 pages of text. **You can do more,** but doing less will impact your score/grade. See Rubric.

Each image will need to be labeled & numbered underneath to credit the artist like this below:

1. *Starry Night* by Vincent Van Gogh, oil on canvas, 1889, Style: Post Impressionism.
[Number, Title, Name of Artist, Material, Year, & Style]

Formatting:

- Single Spaced
- 12 point Arial or Times Font
- 1 empty line between paragraphs
- No indenting
- 1 inch margins all the way around.
- Cover page with title, name, & period does not count in the text requirement.
- Story should equal **AT LEAST** 2 full pages of text.

Image Selection:

- DO NOT use images/illustrations already used in stories/literature.
- Work must be from historically significant artists.
- You may use up to ONE image from a living artist who has work in at least one museum.
- You may use any other form of art like paintings, drawings, sculpture.
- Images DO NOT have to be from the same artist, style, material, theme. Mixing is okay.

Fact Sheet:

At the end of your writing, you will need to research and provide facts about the art and the artist you used for your images. Facts should be in complete sentences. Short or incomplete facts will not count.

- 3 Facts about each artwork
- 3 facts about the artist who made the artwork*
- *If one artist is used for 4 artworks, then you will have a total of 12 facts for that particular artist. (3 x 4 = 12) Choosing one artist does not simplify the writing requirement.

Pre-Planning:

Your writing needs to have 4 major components that will be assessed. *Write notes below.*

1. Characters: Who

2. Setting: Where, When

3. Plot: rising action – the story, the journey, leading to the climax – (The win, loss, or discovery)

4. Resolution: Stories do not need to have a happy ending, but they can.

5 Worksheet: Complete the worksheet on the next page. It is important to number your selected artworks so that everything stays in order. You may change selections if you find better images as you work, but erase and change your pre-work. This pre-work will provide evidence of your depth of knowledge. It is important to include it for the highest assessment possible.

Image Planning Sheet:

Create a simple sketch in each box. Label it. (4 minimum, 6 maximum)

1. Title: **Artist:**	**2. Title:** **Artist:**
3. Title: **Artist:**	**4. Title:** **Artist:**
5. Title: Artist:	6. Title: Artist:

Fact Sheet: (Facts must be full sentences/complete thoughts)

Artwork 1: *Title:* ______________________________

Fact 1. ______________________________

Fact 2. ______________________________

Fact 3. ______________________________

Artist *Name* ______________________________

Fact 1. ______________________________

Fact 2. ______________________________

Fact 3. ______________________________

Artwork 2: *Title:* ______________________________

Fact 1. ______________________________

Fact 2. ______________________________

Fact 3. ______________________________

Artist *Name* ______________________________

Fact 1. ______________________________

Fact 2. ______________________________

Fact 3. ______________________________

Artwork 3: *Title:* ______________________________

Fact 1. ______________________________

Fact 2. ______________________________

Fact 3. ______________________________

Artist *Name* ______________________________

Fact 1. ______________________________

Fact 2. ______________________________

Fact 3. ______________________________

Artwork 4: *Title:* ______________________________

Fact 1. ______________________________

Fact 2. ______________________________

Fact 3. ______________________________

Artist *Name* ______________________________

Fact 1. ______________________________

Fact 2. ______________________________

Fact 3. ______________________________

Please grade your own writing with the rubric below by underlining items.

	100 Exceeds Expectations	90 Meets all requirements	80 Meets most requirements	70 Meets some requirements	60 Meets few requirements	Zero Little or no evidence
Characters	Well considered and added layers of meaning to the story. Personal connections were also evident.	Characters all had purpose and served the story well.	Characters mostly had purpose but some were less resolved than others.	The characters seemed disconnected to the story and some served no real purpose to the plot.	Though present, they did not seem to be appropriate to the story. Disconnected and perhaps distracting.	Not well considered or included in the development of the story.
Setting	Well considered and added layers of meaning to the story. It was described in rich detail. Personal connections were also evident.	Environment had purpose and served the story well. Some details were included to liven the environment.	Environment had a purpose but less resolved or lacking details that would have made it feel more rich or real.	The environment seemed disconnected to the story and some served no real purpose to the plot.	Though present, it did not seem to be appropriate to the story. Disconnected and perhaps distracting.	Not well considered or included in the development of the story.
Plot	ORIGNIAL and well considered and added layers of meaning to the story. It engaged the reader the entire time with unique details or twists with purpose.	Fairly original and well considered. It engaged the reader most of the time. The actions served the story well and made sense.	A bit derivative (*based on another story*) but well considered. It engaged the reader some of the time. The sequence made sense.	The plot seemed derivative, or lacked originality, or had confusing plot-holes, but the sequence of events mostly made sense.	The plot was difficult to follow and was missing important details to help the reader understand the sequence of events.	Not well considered or included in the development of the story.
Resolution	Well considered and meaningful to the story. It was described in rich detail with a deeper message. Personal connections and point of view were also evident.	The ending had purpose and served the story well. There was a message or moral purpose in the end.	The ending had a purpose but less resolved or lacking details that would have made it feel connected or purposeful.	The ending seemed disconnected to the story and not well tied to the purpose of the plot.	The ending did not seem to be connected to the story. Disconnected and perhaps distracting.	Not well considered or included in the development of the story.
Formatting & connected to selected artworks.	Exceeded the required length. Good editing & proof-reading. Work flows beautifully. Art choices feel naturally & fully integrated into the story in the details.	Met the required length & formatting. Proofreading is evident in the lack of common errors. Artwork is solidly connected to the story.	Missed length or formatting details. Work could have been improved by proofreading. The selected images are connected to the story though loosely.	Missed length & formatting details. Proofreading would have helped. The images lack strong connections to the story.	Too short and not formatted. Lack of proofreading is evident. The images are not well connected to the story but are included.	No attempt was made to proofread or organize content at all. Careless and unfocused use of images.
Fact Sheet	More than 3 facts ea. about the artist &/or artwork	3 facts ea. about the artist & artwork	2 facts missing or short.	4 facts missing or short	Many facts missing or short	No fact sheet

Recorded Grade ____________ Comments ____

____

Schools Of Art - Introduction

Video Support: https://bit.ly/SchoolsOfArt

Let's find out more about the schools of art. Using textbooks, the internet, or library. Try to complete as much of this information as you can.

1. Renaissance: Dates:___________

Definition:

What is special or unique about this school of art?

Two Artists: ________________________ & ______________________

2. Baroque: Dates: _______________

Definition:

What is special or unique about this school of art?

Two Artists: ________________________ & ______________________

3. Rococo: Dates: _______________

Definition:

What is special or unique about this school of art?

Two Artists: ________________________ & ______________________

4. Neo-Classical: Dates: ________________

Definition:

What is special or unique about this school of art?

Two Artists: __________________________ & ________________________

5. Romanticism: Dates: ________________

Definition:

What is special or unique about this school of art?

Two Artists: __________________________ & ________________________

6. Realism : Dates ________________

Definition:

What is special or unique about this school of art?

Two Artists: __________________________ & ________________________

7. Impressionism : Dates _______________

Definition:

What is special or unique about this school of art?

Two Artists: _________________________ & _______________________

8. Expressionism: Dates _______________

Definition:

What is special or unique about this school of art?

Two Artists: _________________________ & _______________________

9. Cubism: Date _______________ (*This one is an exact year*)

Definition:

What is special or unique about this school of art?

Two Artists: _________________________ & _______________________

10. Dada: Dates _______________

Definition:

What is special or unique about this school of art?

Two Artists: _________________________ & ________________________

11. Surrealism: Dates _______________

Definition:

What is special or unique about this school of art?

Two Artists: _________________________ & ________________________

12. Abstract Expressionism: Dates _______________

Definition:

What is special or unique about this school of art?

Two Artists: _________________________ & ________________________

13. Pop art: Dates _______________

Definition:

What is special or unique about this school of art?

Two Artists: _________________________ & _______________________

14. What style seems the most interesting and why?

____

____

____

15. What painting did you see that you liked the most and why?

____

____

____

Schools of Art Overview

Write 3 facts about each.

Renaissance

1. ______________________________
2. ______________________________
3. ______________________________

Baroque

1. ______________________________
2. ______________________________
3. ______________________________

Rococo

1. ______________________________
2. ______________________________
3. ______________________________

Neo-Classical

1. ______________________________
2. ______________________________
3. ______________________________

Romanticism

1. ______________________________
2. ______________________________
3. ______________________________

Realism

1. ______________________________
2. ______________________________
3. ______________________________

Impressionism

1. ______________________________
2. ______________________________
3. ______________________________

Cubism

1. ______________________________
2. ______________________________
3. ______________________________

Dada

1. ______________________________
2. ______________________________
3. ______________________________

Surrealism

1. ______________________________
2. ______________________________
3. ______________________________

Expressionism

1. ______________________________
2. ______________________________
3. ______________________________

Abstract Expressionism

1. ______________________________
2. ______________________________
3. ______________________________

Pop Art

1. ______________________________
2. ______________________________
3. ______________________________

Tutorials: https://bit.ly/SchoolsOfArt

Teacher Only Resource: https://youtu.be/LNYhmO7Dfxs

Schools of Art List

Video Support: https://bit.ly/SchoolsOfArt

Renaissance – French word for "rebirth," This work showed Greek, Roman or Bible stories, they tried to make the work look 3-D with perspective. It is the oldest style we need to know, and looks old. Some artists would include Leonardo da Vinci, Michelangelo, (and the other Ninja Turtles. 1400-1500s

Baroque – Looks like it might be on stage and have a spotlight. Look for drama in the action or the lighting. Often has very dark and very light areas, but not always. You might see Musketeer's style clothes of the 1600s.

Rococo – Sickeningly Sweet, everything is rosy and RICH, it shows people playing. Cute and fluffy were their main ideas. Rococo is like Baroque but topped off with a tub of sugar. Look for Cinderella style dresses. Early 1700s

Neo-Classical –Rococo's opposite. The Neo-Classical artists were trying to kick out the King and queen. The paintings are VERY organized, serious, often with big shapes hidden in the paintings. These paintings often included Greek and Roman images so be careful to not confuse it with Renaissance. Most buildings in Washington DC are examples of this style. During the French and American revolutions.

Romanticism – In the early 1800s, it usually showed man and nature but not always peaceful. Sometimes man is using nature—like hills or mountains to fight a war, or hunt to feed his family, but man is never hurting nature in this work, the opposite may be true. If images include slaves, it's probably the next style...

Realism –Is what it sounds like. Realism showed the good and the bad. It began before there were cameras, so the artists tried to paint as much detail as they could. Today, some of these paintings look like photographs. Before, people were usually painted prettier than they were. Middle 1800s

Impressionism – Started in France in the 1860's, the artists tried to paint to show how

Cont...

important light is. Monet, Cassatt, Van Gogh, Cézanne, and Pissaro are Impressionist painters These paintings are usually THICK with paint. Paintings are made while looking at what you are painting. Many of these paintings have a "Z" pattern hiding inside them. Late 1800s

Cubism – Started by Pablo Picasso with his painting in 1907 of Demoiselles d'Avignon. Usually the art looks shattered, and broken into shapes like broken glass, but you can still see what's going on.

NOT ALL work with shapes is CUBISM!

Expressionism – These paintings must have images you can understand but it is a little weird, or very strange to express emotions. All art should show emotion, the artists of this school of art use color or shape to help make the emotions stand out. Edvard Munch is an artist of this style. 1920s

Abstract Expressionism – NO pictures can be seen. The work looks like splashes, or layers of color, or child-like. *If you can't tell at all what's going on in the painting it is probably this style.* 1940s

Dada – A strange art movement that started in Germany in the early 1920's. The artists tried to make fun of art and the people who liked museum art. They would make things that most people thought was junk, or not "real" art, like a toilet up-side-down. Marcel DuChamp is a famous artist of this style. 1920s

Surrealism – Started in the 1920's and was often about dreams or the secrets in your brain. Art in the Surrealist style often looked dreamlike or impossible. Some artists were De Chirico, Salvador Dali, Rene Magritte, and Joan Míro.

Pop Art – Started in New York in the 1950s and 60s, a style of art that comes from popular culture including stuff you buy in a store (like soup or soda), commercials, simple every-day stuff, and cartoons. Some famous artists Keith Haring, Claes Oldenburg, and Andy Warhol.

Important art to remember

Pablo Picasso, **1907** of *Demoiselles d'Avignon.*

The painting above is the first painting in human history that a person was painted in a way that was different on purpose. They style is called Cubism, it was the first one! **Below** is the *Mona Lisa*, by Leonardo Da Vinci, a Renaissance Artist from the late 1400s. It is the most famous painting in the world!

The painting to the right →
…is a painting of a dream. The stuff in the painting is not real, but it is painted to look very real. This is called surrealism.

Starry Night, by Vincent VanGogh,

The painting above is special too, because the artist starts to use color to express his feelings. It is an Impressionist painting but some people call it post-impressionism.

Christina's World (above) by Andrew Wyeth is an example of Realism. It shows a lot of detail, and had both good things and bad things in the painting. People think it is a young girl, but it is really older lady named… Christina.

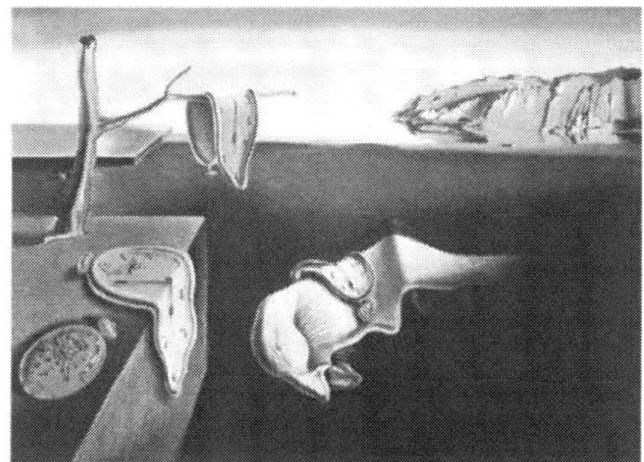

Persistence of Memory by Salvador Dali

Art History Flowchart

START HERE

Question	Answer	Next	Answer	Style
Is there a subject? Can you see "stuff" you recognize?	No	Check the title, are you sure there is no subject?	Yes	**Abstract Expressionism**
			No	Start Over
Yes				
Are people wearing togas? (*Roman Robes or capes*) If there are nudes, do they look like the kind you might see in church art?	Yes	Are their poses relaxed or very dramatic?	Relaxed	**Renaissance**
			Dramatic	**Neoclassical**
No				
Is there anything impossible, magical, or "dream-like" happening?	Yes	**Surrealism**		
No				
Is there a strong sense of emotion in the art and do the colors, shapes, or textures help make that stronger? **OR** does it have a very unusual use of shape, form, color, or texture that almost hides the subject?	Yes	Do you see obvious geometric shapes or shattered images?	Yes	**Cubism**
			No	**Expressionism**
No				
Does it include images from popular culture of regular common stuff with bold color that wouldn't normally be considered art?	Yes	Did it take effort to make?	Yes	**Pop Art**
			No	**Dada**
No				
Does it show very rich or royal people playing or being naughty? Do even the trees and clothes look rich and fluffy?	Yes	**Rococo**		
No				
Is the background very dark but you see dramatic spot-lighting? Is it old fashioned with clothing of the 1600s like from the 3 Musketeers or Pirates of the Caribbean	Yes	**Baroque**		
No				
Is the paint thick and obvious and could it have been painted from observation?	Yes	**Impressionism**		
No				
Do you see hunting, hiking, or farming? (People formally interacting with nature)	Yes	Are the people working or might they be slaves?	Yes	**Realism**
			No	**Romanticism**
No				
Is it dramatic, like showing a fight or something that may cause death?	Yes	**Romanticism**		
No				
Does it look a photograph?	Yes	**Realism**		
No				
It might be a style not on this chart.				

www.FirehousePublications.com

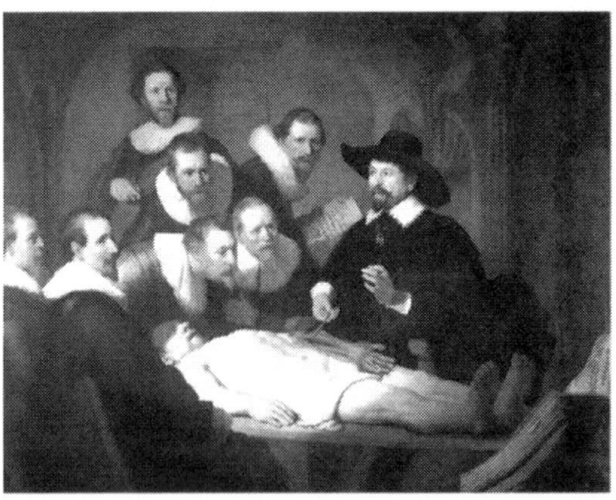

Schools of Art: Matching

Circle the description and draw a line to the image it belongs to.

Baroque: Highly organized and posed; Dramatic lighting like a spotlight: Older style but people wear the clothes of their time. People are not made to look better than they really are, so it's a bit more realistic. Musketeer style clothing.

Neoclassical: Highly organized and dramatic. Often includes a morality message. Created to look grand and important. People in the images often wear togas.

Renaissance: People in these images often wear togas but have relaxed poses. Though organized it is less dramatic than the other styles above. Often include themes from the Bible or mythology. Sometimes has hints of perspective.

Rococo: Usually includes images of the royalty of the time or the very rich. People in the images are often just playing or being a bit naughty. There is no morality message except to have fun. Trees and elements in the pictures have an overly "fluffy" appearance. Sickeningly sweet.

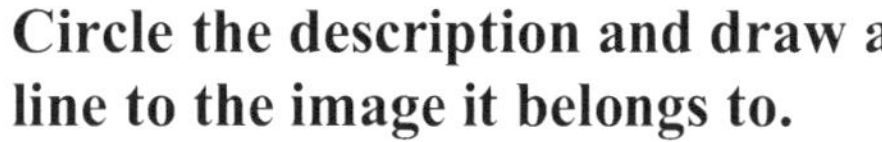

Circle the description and draw a line to the image it belongs to.

Dada: Art that looks the least like "ART." Sometimes considered absurd or an insult to art. Sometimes artists used simple common objects or random objects to be their art. It was very controversial but was a springboard for Pop Art which came later and is sometimes called *Neo-Dada.*

Romanticism: *NOT* about love, but the idea of man and nature together. Sometimes nature dominates man, and sometimes they coexist harmoniously. Man NEVER dominates nature in these images.

Realism: Is as it sounds, realistic. Images are created with attention to detail and showing things as they really are with their flaws and beauty. Sometimes this work has obvious brushstrokes, sometimes not. If it looks like a photograph it is likely this style or another called "photo-realism."

Circle the description and draw a line to the image it belongs to.

Surrealism: Sometimes very realistic but somehow impossible or dream-like. The style was developed based on psychological examination of dreams and symbols. Some of the work can be humorous, others can be haunting.

Pop Art: Generally colors are bold and vibrant. Images may be based on commercial products, common objects, cartoons, or images from popular culture. It is sometimes called *Neo-Dada*.

Cubism: Images often look shattered or reinterpreted with a geometric look. The subject is generally evident but is abstracted.

Circle the description and draw a line to the image it belongs to.

Abstract Expressionism: NO RECOGNIZABLE IMAGERY CAN BE SEEN. The meaning of the painting is derived from the colors, shapes, textures, or other art elements that the artist has chosen to manipulate. If you see something in the image, like an actual object (cat, cup, person) IT IS NOT THIS STYLE.

Expressionism: The artist uses one or more art elements (*color, shape, form...*) to express heightened emotions in the work. Joy, Anger, Pain, Love are some typical themes. In this style the subject can be easily seen though it may be a bit abstracted because of the expressive technique.

Impressionism: Concerned with the changing effects of light and depicting light. The work often includes bold brush strokes and textures. Sometimes a "Z" pattern can be seen within the work. Images are usually created from observation. Many paintings were created outdoors, but there are portraits, still lives, and more in this style.

Teacher: Though strictly speaking Van Gogh was a Post Impressionist, I feel that on a pre-college level it is helpful to express him as an Impressionist as he displays the key qualities of Impressionism in an exaggerated way.

ABSTRACT is a term to mean "changed from reality." This can be slight or dramatic. ***Abstract is NOT a school of art, but a vocabulary term.*** When paired with expressionism it means the work has no visually recognizable imagery. Abstraction can be slight to extreme; we can see this below.

Realistic Photo Slight Abstraction Strong Abstraction VERY Abstracted

REMEMBER, if there is a subject, then the art is based on a real thing, and it cannot be abstract expressionism. How about below? Is there a subject?

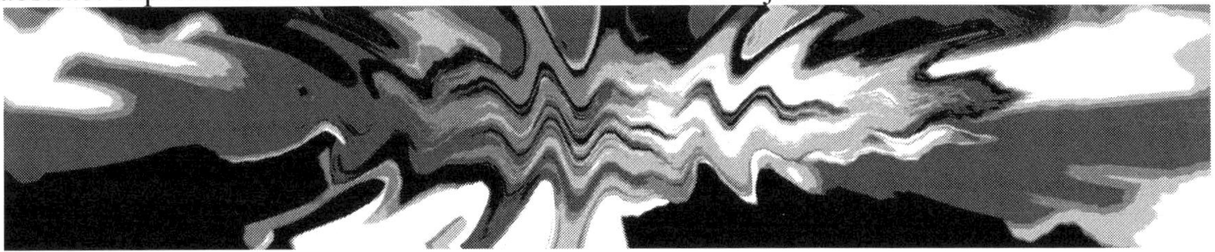

Your teacher will be able to show you many famous painting samples. Decide what school of art they belong to based on clues you see within the artwork.

Sketch Below:

What school of art do you believe it to be from?

____

What 3 pieces of evidence can you see?

1. ____________________________
2. ____________________________
3. ____________________________

What was the real answer?

____

If you were wrong, what did you miss?

____

Student Workbook has 6 pages like this

Sketch Below:

What school of art do you believe it to be from?

____

What 3 pieces of evidence can you see?

1. ___________________________

2. ___________________________

3. ___________________________

What was the real answer?

____

If you were wrong, what did you miss?

____

Sketch Below:

What school of art do you believe it to be from?

____

What 3 pieces of evidence can you see?

1. ___________________________

2. ___________________________

3. ___________________________

What was the real answer?

____

If you were wrong, what did you miss?

____

Reflection/Closure

Date: ________: ________________

____

Date: ________: ________________

____

Date: ________: ________________

____

Date: ________: ________________

____

Student books have two pages like this where they can write reflections about the day at the end of class to fulfill closure requirements. The teacher can prompt a different response each day appropriate to the daily focus.

Some closure questions may include:

- What do you still have questions about?
- What terms did we learn today?
- What do you need to do to finish on time?
- How can you improve your project?
- What safety issues do we need to remember?
- How can your partner improve their project?
- What other course does this project relate to?

On the following pages note your closure question of the day for future reference, or should an administrator need evidence of your work.

Date: ________: ________________

____

Date: ________: ____

Date: ________: ____

Date: ________: ____

Date: ________: ____

Date: ________: ____

Date: ________: ____

Date: ________: ____

Date: ________: ____

Date: ________: ____

Date: ________: ____

Reflection/Closure

Date: ________: ____

Date: ________: ____

Date: ________: ____

Date: ________: ____

Date: ________: ____

Date: ________: ____

Date: ________: ____

Date: ________: ____

Date: ________: ____

Date: ________: ____

Date: ________: ____

Date: ________: ____

Date: ________: ____

Date: ________: ____

Date: ________: ____

Date: ________: ____

Date: ________: ____

Date: ________: ____

Date: ________: ____

Date: ________: ____

Written Assignment Literacy Rubric

______________________________ ___/___/___

Literacy Element	20	17	15	12	10
Clear: Coherent Understandable					
Cohesive: On topic Focused, Factual					
Complete: Sentences Simple/Complex Length					
Comprehensive: Depth Original/Personal					
Correct: Grammar Spelling & Punctuation					

20=Mastery, 17=Proficient, 15=Expected, 12=Approach, 10=Misses

Notes:

Written Assignment Literacy Rubric

______________________________ ___/___/___

Literacy Element	20	17	15	12	10
Clear: Coherent Understandable					
Cohesive: On topic Focused, Factual					
Complete: Sentences Simple/Complex Length					
Comprehensive: Depth Original/Personal					
Correct: Grammar Spelling & Punctuation					

20=Mastery, 17=Proficient, 15=Expected, 12=Approach, 10=Misses

Notes:

Written Assignment Literacy Rubric

______________________________ ___/___/___

Literacy Element	20	17	15	12	10
Clear: Coherent Understandable					
Cohesive: On topic Focused, Factual					
Complete: Sentences Simple/Complex Length					
Comprehensive: Depth Original/Personal					
Correct: Grammar Spelling & Punctuation					

20=Mastery, 17=Proficient, 15=Expected, 12=Approach, 10=Misses

Notes:

Written Assignment Literacy Rubric

______________________________ ___/___/___

Literacy Element	20	17	15	12	10
Clear: Coherent Understandable					
Cohesive: On topic Focused, Factual					
Complete: Sentences Simple/Complex Length					
Comprehensive: Depth Original/Personal					
Correct: Grammar Spelling & Punctuation					

20=Mastery, 17=Proficient, 15=Expected, 12=Approach, 10=Misses

Notes:

The following assignment is meant to show growth in student literacy in art. Writing can be done weekly or bi-weekly as an exercise paired with the "Written Assignment Literacy Rubric." Prompts below images will help students deepen their analysis of the work. **Students should see large color versions of these images before writing.**

1. Compare and Contrast these two famous works of art.

This should be a short writing assignment to help me see where your abilities are right now.

Mona Lisa by Leonardo da Vinci

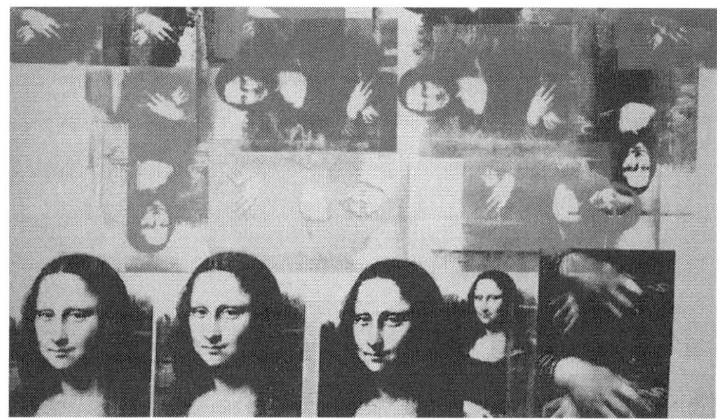

Andy Warhol's *Mona Lisa*

2. Compare and contrast these two famous works of art.

Christina's World by Andrew Wyeth & *Wanderer Above the Sea of Fog* by Caspar D. Friedrich

Checklist:

1. Take time to describe the images first including 3 key descriptions each.
2. Include at least 3 similarities and 3 differences in the work.

3. Compare and contrast these two famous artworks.

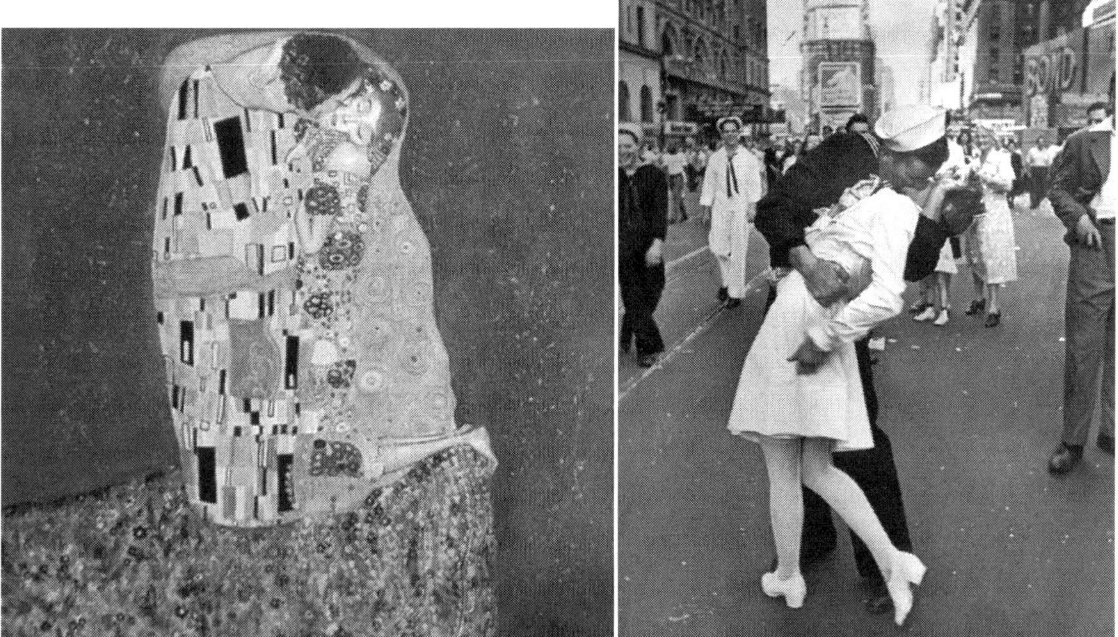

The Kiss by Gustav Klimt and *Vj Day* (End of World War 2) a photograph by Alfred Eisenstaedt

Checklist:

1. Take time to describe the images first including 3 key descriptions each.
2. Include at least 3 similarities and 3 differences in the work.
3. USE at least 3 art vocabulary items within your writing (Elements/Principles)
4. What is each artist trying to say/express, describing the mood/tone within each work?

4. Compare and contrast these two famous artworks.

The Potato Eaters by Vincent van Gogh (An early work), and *Starry Night* by van Gogh

Checklist:

1. Take time to describe the images first including 3 key descriptions each.
2. Include at least 3 similarities and 3 differences in the work.
3. USE at least 3 art vocabulary items within your writing (Elements/Principles)
4. What is the artist trying to say/express, describing the mood/tone within each work?
5. Include a personal connection within your writing to one or both of the artworks.
6. Include at least one fact from the artist's life to each work.
7. Describe the evolution, progress, or growth of the artist from one work to the other.

This essay should show your growth in writing. Take your time, review and edit your work. Have a classmate read and review your writing as well. Review a second time and complete edits.

Video Notes

Video notes are an essential part of your grade and the easiest "A's" you will ever earn... Sometimes the teacher will be here for these videos, BUT a teacher does not need to be here to push "play" on a DVD. These assignments are mostly given when the teacher is out of school for a conference or something. These assignments are to help you learn about Art History, a mandatory part of all art classes.

The teacher could assign readings within a textbook and written assignments… or you could do a video once in a while…

Some videos will be short, but most will take a whole period. To earn your 100% for a full period video, all you need is 20 facts about what you see unless otherwise stated. Facts can be things you hear the artist or moderator say, but they can also be things you observe in the video. Mainly the teacher needs to see evidence that you have watched the video and paid attention. **Two word facts are NOT acceptable.** Most students can get all the notes before the video is even half over. There is no excuse for not completing these assignments and getting 100%.

IF you are absent for the video, you will be excused from the assignment. Your name MUST appear as absent on the school's attendance roster. You may use a "Pass Point" instead of doing the notes, but this is a waste of a VALUABLE opportunity to raise a test grade. You will never be pestered into doing these assignments… it is after all, your own grade.

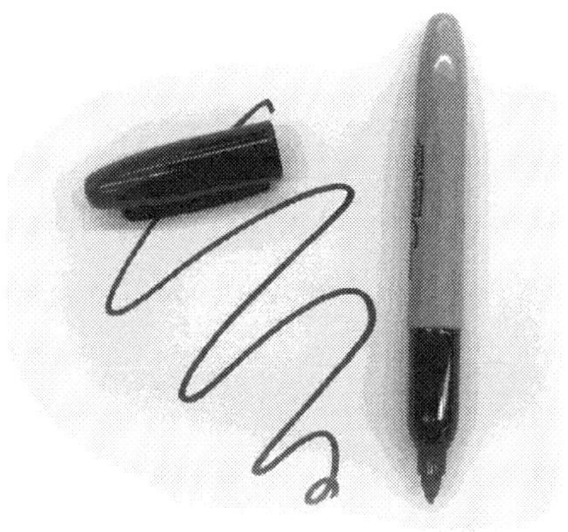

Student Workbook has 4 pages like this

Short Video Notes (Vimo/Youtube) **Title or Topic** ____________________________

Note 5 facts or interesting observations about the video.

1. ____

2. ____

3. ____

4. ____

5. ____

Reflecting on the video, what did you find most interesting, unique, or thought provoking?

____

____

____

Short Video Notes (Vimo/Youtube) **Title or Topic** ____________________________

Note 5 facts or interesting observations about the video.

1. ____

2. ____

3. ____

4. ____

5. ____

Reflecting on the video, what did you find most interesting, unique, or thought provoking?

____

____

____

Student Workbook has 8 pages like this

VIDEO NOTES – GRADED ASSIGNMENT

TITLE_______________________________

Period___ Date __/__/__

Directions: Write 20 facts below based on the video WHILE YOU WATCH. ***Two word facts, silliness, and incomplete thoughts will not be acceptable.*** *This is GRADED as part of 10% of your quarter's grade.*

1. ____
2. ____
3. ____
4. ____
5. ____
6. ____
7. ____
8. ____
9. ____
10. ____
11. ____
12. ____
13. ____
14. ____
15. ____
16. ____
17. ____
18. ____
19. ____
20. ____

Summarize the video. What is the main idea or what can you infer? (10 pts.)

____

____

____

Double check that all facts have MORE than 2 words.

GRADED BY TEACHER: FULL CREDIT 100% OR ________________% Credit

Mid-Project Peer Review

Artwork by: ______________________

Peer Partner: ______________________

What is going well in the project? ______________________

____

____

What are some specific areas that are missing, unresolved, or need more attention?

____

____

What are some ideas to improve the project *OR* areas the artist should pay attention to?

____

____

____

What resources can be used if the artist gets "stuck" along the way? Who/what can help?

____

____

- -

Mid-Project Peer Review

Artwork by: ______________________

Peer Partner: ______________________

What is going well in the project? ______________________

____

____

What are some specific areas that are missing, unresolved, or need more attention?

____

____

What are some ideas to improve the project *OR* areas the artist should pay attention to?

____

____

____

What resources can be used if the artist gets "stuck" along the way? Who/what can help?

____

____

Mid-Project Peer Review

Artwork by: ______________________

Peer Partner: ______________________

What is going well in the project? ______________________________________

____

____

What are some specific areas that are missing, unresolved, or need more attention?

____

____

What are some ideas to improve the project *OR* areas the artist should pay attention to?

____

____

____

What resources can be used if the artist gets "stuck" along the way? Who/what can help?

____

____

- -

Mid-Project Peer Review

Artwork by: ______________________

Peer Partner: ______________________

What is going well in the project? ______________________________________

____

____

What are some specific areas that are missing, unresolved, or need more attention?

____

____

What are some ideas to improve the project *OR* areas the artist should pay attention to?

____

____

____

What resources can be used if the artist gets "stuck" along the way? Who/what can help?

____

____

Project Reflection:

Title: ______________________________ Media ________________

Explanation of the project goals: ______________________________

____

Description:

____

____

____

Connections (To Self, Community, Culture, or traditions) ________________

____

____

My process: ____

____

____

Knowledge I had and applied to this project: ____________________

____

____

Something new I learned or "figured out" through this project: ______________

____

____

The most successful part of this project was… ____________________

____

____

If I had to do it over again, I would… ________________________

____

____

I hope when others view my work… ________________________

____

____

Project Reflection: *(Student edition has 4 of these pages)*

Title: ________________________________ Media ________________

Explanation of the project goals: ______________________________

____

Description:

____

____

____

Connections (To Self, Community, Culture, or traditions) ______________

____

____

My process: ____

____

____

Knowledge I had and applied to this project: _____________________

____

____

Something new I learned or "figured out" through this project: __________

____

____

The most successful part of this project was… _____________________

____

____

If I had to do it over again, I would… _________________________

____

____

I hope when others view my work… ___________________________

____

____

Project Reflection 2

Title: ________________________________ **Media** ______________________

Description: (***Describe your work as if you were talking over the phone***)

____

____

____

____

____

Describe the main art elements you used. (Line, Shape, Form, Color, Value, Light, Texture.) Write in such a way that it is clear you understand the art elements.

____

____

____

____

Describe the main art principles you used. (Contrast, Unity, Balance, Emphasis, Variety, Movement, Pattern.) Write in such a way that it is clear you understand the art principles.

____

____

____

____

(Peer Name) ____________________ **said the most successful part of my project was…**

____

____

____

____

(Peer Name) ____________________ **suggested if I had to do it over again, I should…**

____

____

____

____

Project Reflection 2 *(The student edition has 4 of these pages)*

Title: ______________________________ **Media** ____________________

Description: **(*Describe your work as if you were talking over the phone*)**

____

____

____

____

____

Describe the main art elements you used. (Line, Shape, Form, Color, Value, Light, Texture.) Write in such a way that it is clear you understand the art elements.

____

____

____

____

Describe the main art principles you used. (Contrast, Unity, Balance, Emphasis, Variety, Movement, Pattern.) Write in such a way that it is clear you understand the art principles.

____

____

____

____

(Peer Name) ____________________ **said the most successful part of my project was…**

____

____

____

____

(Peer Name) ____________________ **suggested if I had to do it over again, I should…**

____

____

____

____

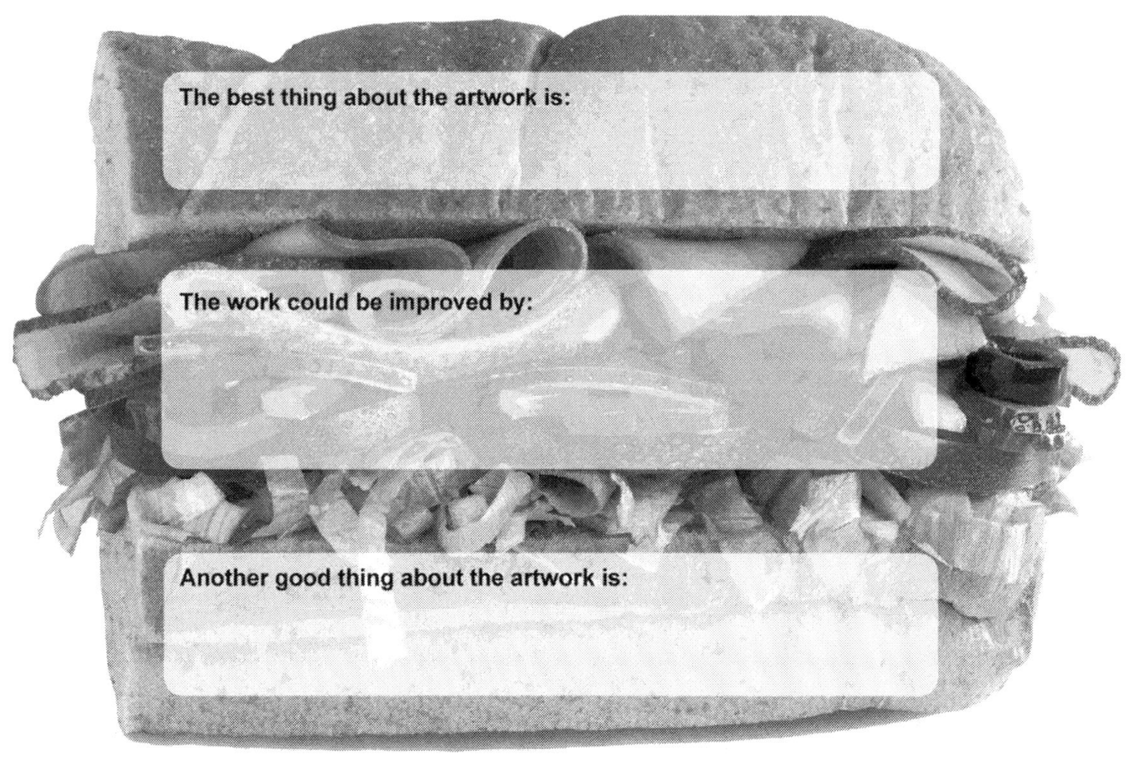
The best thing about the artwork is:
The work could be improved by:
Another good thing about the artwork is:

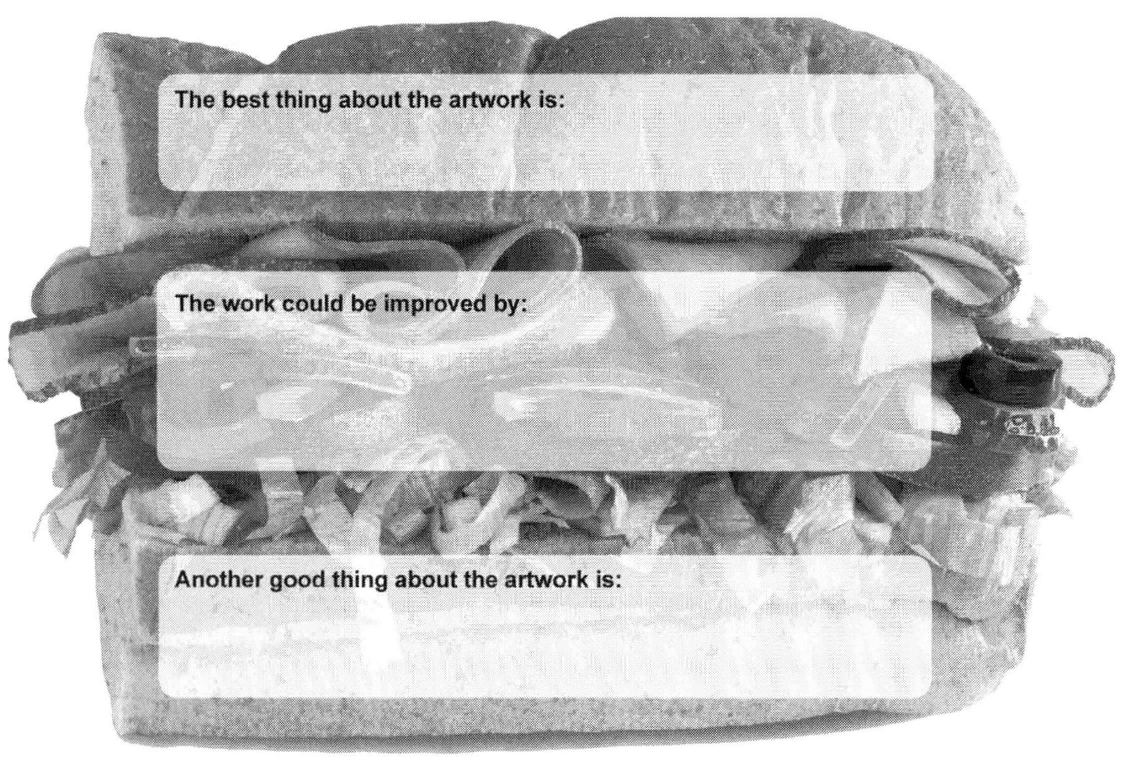
The best thing about the artwork is:
The work could be improved by:
Another good thing about the artwork is:

Formal Critique: *(Student Edition has 3 pages like this)*

Title ____________________________ Artist ________________________ Year _______

Describe the art as if you are explaining it over the phone.

____

____

____

____

Check what you included: [_] Media, [_] Elements, [_] Style/Genre, [_] Objects, [_] Technique

Analysis: Describe how the artist used the art principles.
(Unity, Contrast, Balance, Emphasis, Variety, Movement, Pattern)

____

____

____

____

Interpretation: Use evidence from above to explain the meaning or message of the work.

____

____

____

____

Evaluation: Judge the work explaining why you feel that way. (Is there room for improvement?)

____

____

____

____

Drawing and Painting Project Ideas:

Some lessons can be augmented to work in different media.

Alphabets: [Problem Solving, Literature, History] Students pick a broad theme of their own interest and create an entire alphabet based on that theme. Objects should be in the shape of the letters. See supporting pages and examples in this book. Illuminated Manuscripts are a good historical reference for this project.

Portraits: [Biology, proportion, math] First without any instruction, then as blind drawings, then with exposure to proper proportions and finally with a grid. Students are assigned to bring in a photo of a family member or figure they admire. I have also done this project with a surrealistic component, where students mix a symbol of their personality and merge it with their portrait.

Pop Art Pop: [History, political activism] Students find a common object like a soda can, and re-draw and paint it in as many different modes as possible, blind drawing, contour, blind contour, stipple, crosshatch, color field. All work should be on the same size paper or canvas and when complete, images should be placed side by side to create a Warhol-inspired image. To make this easier, each student can be given a similar object and as a class create a larger mural-like project.

Tessellations: [Geometry, math, tool skills] M.C. Escher. Plenty of support info on the net to do this. I like Crystal Productions' posters for this lesson. A Tessellation is a pattern that repeats infinitely. See example in this book.

Family with Shapes and Colors: [Psychology, problem solving] Students list 8 members of their family and write 5 descriptive words about each. Using the *Color and Shape Expression* worksheet in this book, they create symbolic shapes and colors for each and create a composition to represent their family. Klee and Kandinsky are good samples for work like this.

Jabberwocky: [Literature] Poem in this book. Without showing students any illustrations, they interpret the poem and illustrate one stanza. Work is collected and put on display. Include foreground, middle-ground, background, and overlap. See example in this book.

Cubism Simplified: [Geometry] Using a ruler, criss-cross a page in every possible direction with a pencil or pen. Choose an image from a magazine you like and "Force" the image into these geometric shapes. Seeing Picasso samples is helpful. Lines can also be used less abstractly to divide areas of color. Example on previous page in this book.

Comic Book / Movie Poster Parody: [Literature, career studies] Taking a favorite movie, change the name a bit and create a new image for the parody. Include foreground, middle-ground, background, overlap, title, subtitle, logo, and dramatic action. (see sample in this workbook) See Warhol and Lichtenstein for Pop Art Samples of comic art. See example in this book.

Aboriginal Family Story: [World Cultures] Using samples of aboriginal paintings, and internet samples of aboriginal symbols, create a work that describes an important event from your own family history, recent or old, good or bad. Use the page of expressive shapes and colors to help. Fill all areas with pattern.

Drawings from Observation: [Biology] When weather permits, it is nice to go outside and draw a scene from nature. Make it fun by adding a surrealistic element, changing colors, or exaggerating elements within the scene. In spring-time it is fun to tag a branch when budding with loosely tied yarn, and redrawing that branch as a bloom grows. Andrew Wyeth is a good example artist here.

Teacher Notes:

Compound Word Illustration. "Toad-Stool"

Sun Mandela: [World Cultures] See samples of Asian mandelas and create your own based on the sun as a theme. It can be done in watercolor with oil pastel resist. Consider the use of a cultural tie-in by asking students to use themes found in their own cultural background. Mandelas can also be made by using information from the emotional values of color and shape worksheet. By repeating shapes based on personality traits of themselves or family members they can cut these shapes from oak-tag and repeat them in a radial design. Corners of rectangular paper can be filled in too with the 4 seasons of ourselves either abstractly or with imagery. (FYI: Rubber cement is a good resist media too for bright whites, in well-ventilated area.)

Sunset Silhouette: [Physics/color] Teach students to color blend with sunset colors, overlay black on the bottom quarter to create a land silhouette in black. Add in a tree, a man-made element and person in profile to complete it.

Compound Word Illustration: [English] Create a list of compound words and illustrate them in a way that shows their incorrect meaning. Include foreground, middle-ground, background, and overlap. (Butterfly, a stick of butter flying) See list in book.

Wild World Collage: [History] Collecting images from magazines, kids create crazy combinations of images (Jets with butterfly wings, people with animal legs etc…) All of this is glued down to one large background image. Wavy Gravy is a collage artist of the 60's. Themes can be chosen, like current events or an event in history to create a historical tie-in.

Perspective: [Geometry] One-point perspective of a school hallway. Use rulers and worksheets in this book to prepare for the project. At the end I have students add in 1 surrealistic element to make the scene subtly spooky or funny. (Ninja dropping in from ceiling tile, T-Rex tail coming out a door…) See artists of the Renaissance for good examples of perspective.

Cut-Out Still Life: [Tool skills, history, problem solving] Do a large contour drawing of a simple still life. Behind this layer newspaper, magazines, construction paper, etc… Staple this packet and cut out contours. Reconstruct the still life on a new paper mixing layered cut-outs. Add drawing lines on top for shading and define contours as needed. Picasso and Braque had good examples of work like this.

Environmental Drawing: [Earth Science] Teacher will need to have MANY examples set aside. Students create their own environment (Desert, forest, jungle, coral reef…) and use examples from teacher showing how things should look. No one should draw from imagination but mix and match images from several sources to create one complete image. All elements come from observation of available images. (I get books at Barnes and Noble on super discount, cut them up and laminate the pages) Students are to include foreground, middle-ground, and background.

Dream Drawings: [Psychology and Self Expression] Using J. Miro as an example or Klee, students re-create an image from a persistent dream. Include foreground, middle-ground, and background. See example in book. Discuss Freudian dream symbolism is appropriate.

7 Step Transition: [Geometry] Using a long strip of paper, students draw 2 objects, unrelated to each other, on opposite ends. In 7 steps (including the 2 images) students show a transition or "morph" of one image into the other. (Scissor turning into a coke can in 7 steps.)

Treasure Maps: [Geometry/Geography] Students create a treasure map of an imaginary island. The island can take on the contour of an object, but break it into small pieces so it is not too obvious. Include the following: Detailed border, rose compass, longitude/latitude, 5 land feature symbols, key for symbols, 2 landmarks, 2 water symbols in the water, 1 sea monster and 1 ship. Maps can be aged by wrinkling and soaking in watered-down paint.

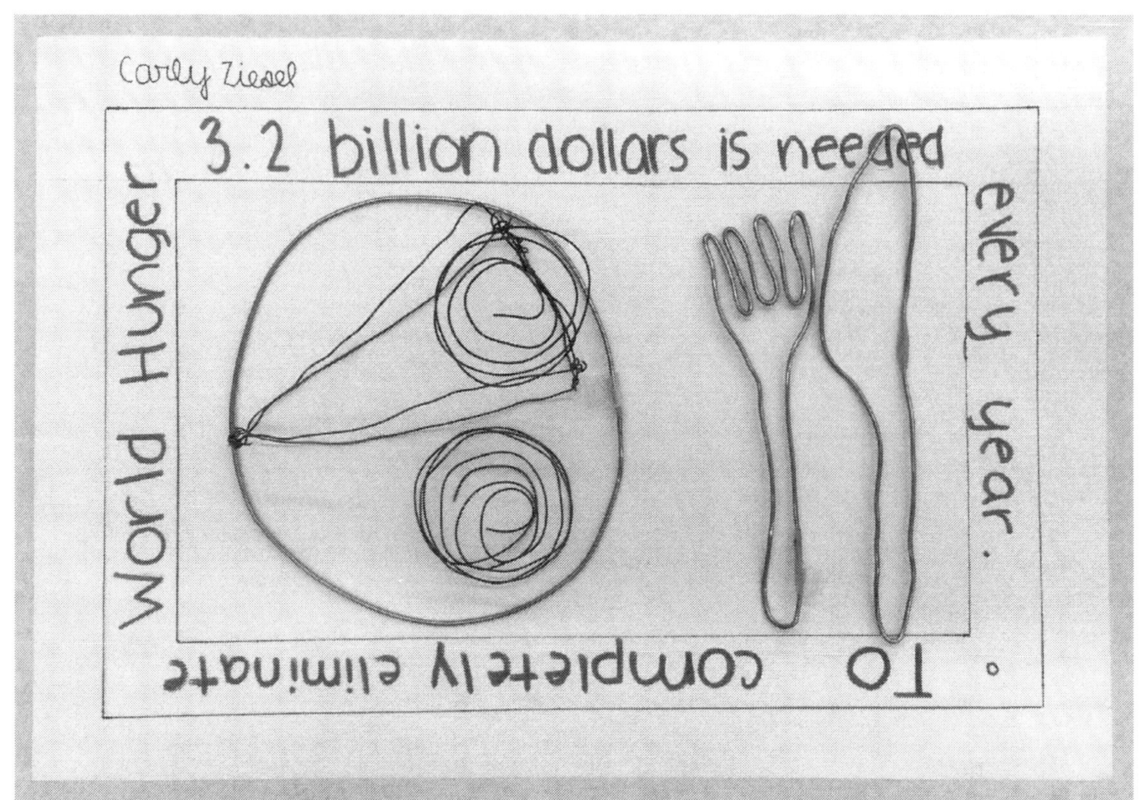

Wire Food Sculpture & Hunger Fact by Carly Ziesel

Shoe Art Projects, entered into the "Vans Custom Culture" contest.

Wrinkle World: [Problem Solving] Take a large piece of paper, wrinkle it into a ball, open and stare at it, and trace shapes you see that make images. This is very similar to watching clouds and trying to see shapes and creatures in them. Color in and make as detailed as possible.

Trompe l'oeil: [History] Students create simple compositions on art-board with 6 - 8 personal symbolic objects. We start with a contour tracing of the board and use rules to measure and draw objects as realistically as possible on a 1-to-1 scale. Layering of colors is stressed as well as adding in realistic tone with regular pencil.

Flower Dissection: [Science] Drawing and labeling with research. Students can gather flowers or bring some in, maybe a donation of old flowers from a flower shop. Students dissect flowers with an X-Acto knife and draw from observation. Later, within the library or computer lab, students label the parts that they have observed. Enlarge sketches and use as references for larger paintings like Georgia O'Keeffe.

Drawings of Decay: [Science] Students can gather soft tissue plants, even lettuce can work and do one sketch a day of the decaying process. This could even be done in the form of a flipbook. Sketches can also follow the various color changes observed in the plant. I would suggest this as a five-minute sketch at the beginning of each class while doing another project. Sketches can later be more fully completed.

Flipbooks: [Science] of science based observations. Similar to drawings of decay, students could also make flip books based on observations of processes like cell division, plant growth, weather movements, etc.

Code Painting: [Math] Students can create a visual code of colors and shapes to represent numbers, letter place-holders, and functions, then illustrate a math concept through these colors, shapes, and composition. Pi as a color code, the quadratic formula, solving for unknown angles, etc. This can result in some very abstract works of art but reinforce the math concepts the students have chosen to base their work on. Images should be examined afterward to see if any larger patterns emerge.

Scavenger Hunt: [History] Students can be given 20 thumbnails of images to find via library resources or the internet. They should label the images as a kind of art history scavenger hunt. This can be taken a step further by requiring that the date of the image be found, the place of creation, and students find an historical event from that time and place to include in their scavenger hunt.

Idioms: [English and Culture Studies] Definition: an expression whose meaning is not predictable from the usual meanings of its constituent elements, as *kick the bucket* or *hang one's head.* Similar to the "My Cultural Background" worksheet, students research their cultural background seeking out idioms particular to their country or language of national origin. They illustrate their chosen idiom in a way that takes the phrase literally, and by sharing with the class the origins and true meaning, teach a bit about their own culture. This can be done as above as a black and white study utilizing hatching techniques, or in nearly any media or mode. We have even done this as a sculpture project with plaster and acrylic paints. (Above: *Hold Your Horses* by Hope Stillwell)

Inside/Outside: [Psychology, World Cultures] Students study the information from the worksheet about the emotional values of color and shape. Then they create a simple silhouette of their profile with a friend tracing their shadow from the sun or light source. The inside is filled with patterns, shapes, and colors that illustrate their internal feelings, and the exterior of the silhouette is filled with color, shape, and pattern to describe how others see them, OR how they view the outside world. This same project can be done as an exploration of culture, using patterns and symbols of their cultures of origin, and outward, symbols of the culture where they now live.

Inside Outside project samples.

Board Game: [History, literature, research skills, writing] Students work in groups to create a board game based on an historical event or time period. Research will help them create playing pieces and images for their board games. Game board can be made with a canvas board or covered cardboard. A game can also be based on something the student is excellent at and knows a lot about, like skateboarding…

Political Cartoon: [Current Events/History] Students could create a political cartoon for a contemporary event or historical one, choosing a side to support for a clear point of view.

Museum Tour: [History] Students can create a diorama of a museum hall setting up an exhibition of images from that particular time. Images should have a companion paper labeled with historical details of the works of art. This can be done for specific schools of art, artists, themes, or based on interests of the students. (ie: finding images of game playing from 8 different centuries). Larger exhibitions can be created as a group project, each group setting up an exhibition in the room for a day or week each.

Art History: [History] Students could take a famous event in human history and create a work of art based on that event. They can even be required to choose a school of art that was from the time of the event from which to create their artwork. (ie: WWI scene in expressionism style.)

Culture Pattern: [World Cultures, Research, Library Skills] Using the "My Cultural Background page, students create a background pattern of objects based on information above found at the library or on the internet. Then cut and paste an animal symbol for themselves on top. Any media will work for this; try colored pencil, marker, or painted paper.

Teacher Notes:

Upper/Lower Coordination: [Community] Pair an upper grade with a lower grade, 3rd grade and Juniors. Have the lower grade students create drawings of the friendly monster they wish they had to protect them from something they don't like. Drawings can be colored in or left black and white. Copy and share these drawings and have upper level students maintain the contours of the original drawing but give it a professional edge, including shading, tone changes, textures, etc. Share and display together.

Artist Trading Cards: [History] Based on samples of baseball or other sports cards on hand, have students create two artist trading cards, one on the artist, one on their work. The list in this book may be used, or create another one. If students pick from a hat, there will be less duplication. Front should include an images of the artist, and the back about their history. A second card should be made of the artists' most famous work, with information about who made it and about the specific work of art. These can be used later in a matching game or as part of an oral presentation.

Blue Period: [History-Theraputic] Students study the work of Picasso understanding the stories behind his blue period and rose period. "The emotional values of color and shape" page, in this workbook will be of help. Have students create self portraits, but rather than realistic colors, use colors that have emotional meaning for how they see themselves. Pattern and shape can also be added with the figure or the background. Mono-print Extension: This same project can also be done as a mono-print unit with the use of mirrors. Have students trace their faces on a mirror with water-based marker. Dampen paper with a spray bottle and press onto the mirror to transfer the image. Color in with emotionally based colors and shapes.

World Hunger: [Social Studies] Students research about facts on world hunger, as a group, decide on an image you feel has great visual impact. Print or create a black and white copy of the image, and break it into a grid assigning pieces to each student. Be sure to note top and bottom. Labeling the backs will help assemble the work later. Darkly toast bread, find a loaf that is very square. Handle each slice of bread as the square of the grid. Scraping the toast will reveal lighter layers. Background toast can be etched with facts on hunger. These can be sprayed with shellac to preserve and put on display.

Surreal Hands: [History] After showing students samples of M.C. Escher's work, particularly his hands drawing hands, have students do a drawing of their hand drawing something they like to eat. Add shadow so it looks convincing.

Shoe Painting:[Recycling and other disciplines] Sometimes painting on an unexpected surface can be a fun motivator for students. Shoes lend themselves to several good projects. They should be primed first and can except a broad range of media. Ask students to bring in one shoe and offer extra credit for bringing in more. I offer 1 extra point for each extra shoe. Spraying the inside of them with Lysol will be helpful. Vans Shoes runs an annual design contest that may lend itself to these projects and win your school $50,000 in school supplies. Search "Vans Custom Culture."

Walk a mile in my shoes: Design your shoes to show off the places you have been and the things you have done that others may not be aware of.

Super Shoes: Create a design that if real would give you the super power you wish you had. What symbols would you include? Should you add wings to the shoes if you'd like to fly?

Inspirational Shoes: Use markers to cover the shoes with an inspirational quote you have them pick from a hat, making some personal connection. Let them trade quotes for the first 5 minutes of class.

Walking Through history: Students draw or paint an historical event on the shoes with images and words. If obtaining old shoes is an issue, often shoe shops dump old stock or donate them. If you present a school's tax ID paperwork, their donation may be tax deductable. Or you can ask everyone to bring in one shoe and give extra credit to those who bring more.

Bug Jars: [Biology, World Cultures] Students research their country of origin finding out what insects are indigenous, and a plant they feel would be easy to draw. Printed samples may be helpful. Trace a jar template onto paper and draw your jar filled with bugs of that country on a plant that is also indigenous. Include a label on the jar indicating the country.

ESL: [English] it may be helpful to partner with your ESL classes for this project. Draw an item and hide the word within the item. For a mouse, M for the ears, O for the body, U for the snout, S for the tail, "e" for the nose. Color in and shade so the letters are still visible but not obvious. Having students draw objects that they relate to will personalize their work. If a student plays the trumpet, that may be the best choice for their illustration. This may be extended by making a larger composition where all the objects are made up of the words they are.

Blended Art: [History] Students research two artists who are very different in style, and create a single painting or image that combines the styles of both artists into one image. Lichtenstein's "Woman with a Hat" is a good example of Cubism and Pop Art.

Cartooning: [Science] Create a comic page illustrating a science concept; cell division, creation of a solar system, etc. Include a super hero to narrate the illustrations. [History] Create a comic page illustrating a point in history. Assign portions to each student so you get a whole graphic novel about a specific historical time period or key event.

Flower Dissection: [Biology] Drawing and labeling with research. Students can gather flowers or bring some in, maybe a donation of old flowers from a flower shop. Students dissect flowers with an X-Acto knife and draw from observation. Later, within the library or computer lab, students label the parts that they have observed. Enlarge sketches and use as references for larger paintings like Georgia O'Keeffe, or to create a Leonardo da Vinci style sketchbook pages.

Fan Letters or Quotes: [English, History] Have students write fan letters to their favorite historical figure, or current celebrity and include a picture of the figure doing something they are most known for or the activity the student admires. Or, have an illustration of the historical figure and include creative text of something they said. It's possible to do the image first and add writing as the border around the image or written within the image—along a road, within the clouds or trees, somewhere that does not obstruct the main image. Celebrity addresses are readily available on the internet. Images can be photographed and sent. Replies can be posted with an image of the artwork that was sent. If done early in the year, enough replies for an exhibition may arrive by the end of the year.

Sidewalk Stories: [Literature] Literature lends itself to illustration, and though it can be done as a traditional painting or drawing, getting students outside for chalk drawing can be a great motivator. Students can spread out over a large area, arranged by chapter, to create an outdoor exhibition of artwork illustrating a particular story. As they work other students can visit their work stations and learn about the work through the students.

Aboriginal Family Story: [World Cultures] Using samples of aboriginal paintings, and internet samples of aboriginal symbols, create a work that describes an important event from your own family history, recent or old, good or bad. Use the page of expressive shapes and colors to help. Fill all areas with pattern.

Teacher Notes:

Sculptural Projects

Some projects may be augmented for clay or to create 2-D projects as drawings or paintings.

Family Mobile: [Geometry/Physics] Students use information from this book about the emotional values of color and shape to create mobiles of their family unit by creating symbolic shapes and colors for each family member and create a composition to represent their family. (8 – 10 shapes recommended) Alexander Calder is a wonderful artist for examples.

Dinosaur Eggs: [Science] Students create dinosaur eggs from plaster and balloons, then crack them open and create a baby dinosaur to fit inside as if in the process of hatching. Students research what their chosen dinosaur would look like as a baby. Eggs and creatures should be related by color to reinforce form and function concepts.

Wire Tree: [World Cultures] Using stovepipe wire or copper, students take 50 to 100 thin strands at about 1 ft in length and twist the wires to make a tree, splitting bunches and twisting roots and branches. Foil, craft jewels, or other leaf-like objects can be added as leaves. See the internet for many examples. Couple this project with research about Bonsai trees and their expressive forms.

Wire People/Portraits: [Biology, history] Using thin wire, students create a self portrait. Include elements unique to themselves. This project can be extended by creating a body as well, doing an activity the student does often, or what they wish to be able to do. Students can create a character from a circus. Alexander Calder did many examples of this too.

Biome House: [Geography/Biology] Show students several biome posters from the biology classes. Environments can be tundra, desert, mountains, grasslands, rain forest, etc. Students choose their favorite; learn a bit more about it, and with foam-core or cardboard, create an architectural cottage or home that would fit within that biome.

Pen of Power: [History/World Cultures] Students take and carve an old branch adding feathers and other natural elements to make a shaman's pen. Students should have a discussion about Native American cultures and create the pen with this in mind. After adding a nib, pens can be used to do a drawing, write a poem, or even create a magical spell.

Monumental Design: [History] Students create a miniature monument to an historic hero, an event they wish they could re-visit, or a monument to a personal achievement, or personal experience. There are many memorials from which to pull examples. See example in book.

Goal and Obstacle: [Career studies, problem solving] Students create lists of life goals and things that may prevent them from these achievements. These lists are converted into symbols. The students then create a work that shows 1 of each. The Obstacle on the bottom as a base and the achievement above. (This can also be done with a box and doing different things with the inside and outside OR combine with the next project of Expressive Heads)

Idioms: [English] Definition: an expression whose meaning is not predictable from the usual meanings of its constituent elements, as *kick the bucket* or *hang one's head.* Students pick an idiom to illustrate as a sculpture in the teacher's chosen media. Inspired by student teacher, Hope Stillwell, in 2013.

Using the "My Cultural Background" worksheet, students can research their cultural background seeking out idioms particular to their country or language of national origin. They illustrate their chosen idiom in a way that takes the phrase literally, and by sharing with the class the origins and true meaning, teach a bit about their own culture.

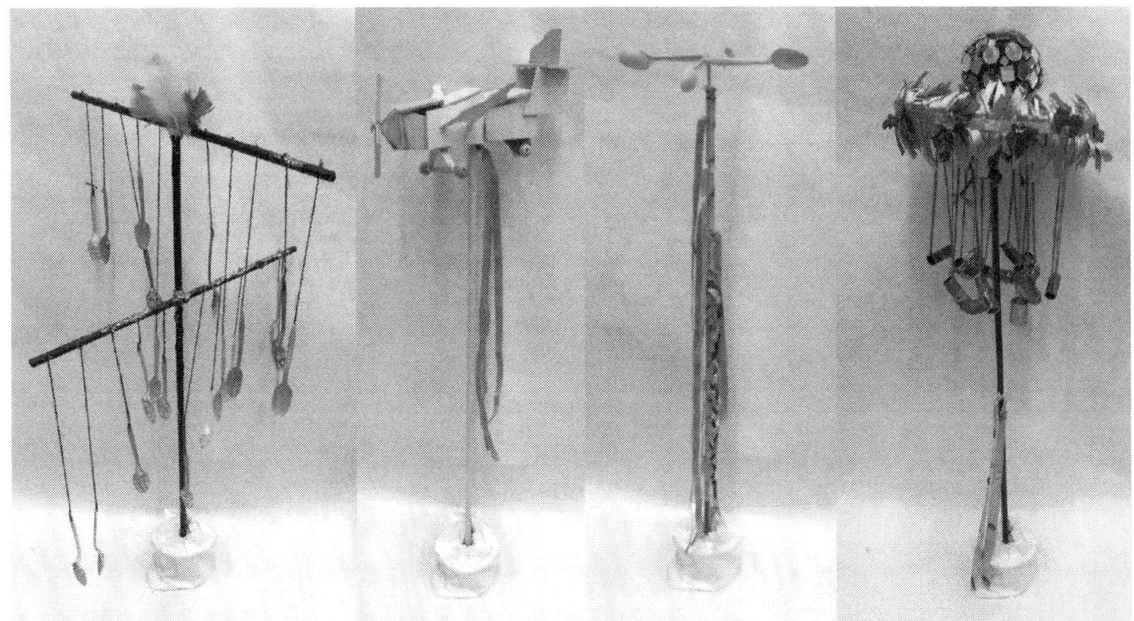
Student Wind Sculptures

Wind Sculptures: [Environmental Science] Using the worksheet in this books students explore the possibilities of wind as an element to sculpt. Students explore current possibilities, flags, whirly-gigs, turbines, chimes, bottles, whistles, streamers, etc. This is also a good project to tie into recycling, I require my student's sculptures be made of 50% or more of recycled materials. We start with a 1/2 inch dowel and build from there, but bamboo or other rod forms can be used as well.

Expressive Head: [History, World Cultures] (I use a foam head from eNasco for this project) Students create a blank head form to cover in a variety of materials to illustrate a personal or social issue they care about. Some ideas: Use magazines and cover the head with words, cover head with a map painting and add pins for places you've visited, destroy head and reassemble, empty head and fill with expressive items, alter the head for expressive reasons. See the artist Robert Arneson for examples. This can also focus on a particular period of time, like ancient Egyptian head sculptures, Aztec sculpture, or those on Easter Island.

Self Portraits: [Problem Solving, Biology] Students create a plaster cast of their faces. Clay is pressed into these to create "Life Masks" which can be painted or glazed with many themes: life story on the face, achievement, my two personalities, inside/outside self, write a poem about the self on the face and others. Plaster mold can also be used to create multiple faces for a larger project, or to create a unique teapot, wall hanging, tile etc… by including pressed clay. See the artist Robert Arneson for examples.

Lippold Crystals: [Geometry] Look up imagery by the artist Lippold. Students create their own crystals with any linear material. I use eNasco acrylic straws, pipe cleaners, and 527 glue. Students start simply and add on structures to make their project grow. They should learn about the necessity of structures that are rigid for project strength. Modular sculptures can be used too, so all work can be combined into a monumental work for display.

Paper Structures: [Physics/Engineering] Students create the tallest tower possible with 4 large sheets of paper and 2 yards of tape. Structure must stand after teacher blows on it. Paper can also be used to design an amusement park, landscape all in white, a house of their dreams. Cardstock can be used to make modular rectangles, like playing cards and glued to create structures.

Teacher Notes:

Environmental Sculptures: [Problem Solving & Engineering] After seeing the work of Andrew Goldsworthy, students create their own environmental sculpture. Students can be broken into smaller groups to make larger structures. Work should be photographed, printed, and displayed.

Pop Art Food: [Problem Solving, history] After seeing the work of Claes Oldenburg, students create their own food sculptures on any scale the teacher requires. They could also sculpt a small everyday item in larger scale with paper or plaster mache. This project can also be done by making paper staple pillows, stuffed with scraps. (Two sheets of paper, stapled 80%, stuff with scraps, and staple closed. Similar to sewing but with staples and paper.)

Anti-Teapot: [Problem Solving, engineering] Create a teapot that does not look like a teapot. It should pour, be able to be held, but the form should be disguised. There are many samples on the internet. Pig teapot, house, dragon, egg, cabbage…

Word Sculpture: [English/Social Studies] Students take a word (Social issue, personal issue or topic they know well) Like "EARTH" and make each letter look like part of the issue you care about. The "E" could be a factory spewing toxins, the "A" could be a hurricane, the "R" could be melting, etc. A list of expressive words in this book may be helpful for topic-based sculptures.

Plaster People: [Problem Solving, Construction, biology] After seeing examples of the work of George Segal, students work in groups to make a plaster cast of a student engaged in a school activity. This sculpture should be placed in the school environment. I suggest casting parts each day and assembling parts at the end and stuffing them with paper. Face, back of head, body trunk, arms, legs. You will need tools to cut plaster safely from the body. Models wear OLD clothes as they will be ruined. Casts can be made in multiple 40-minute periods if well planned.

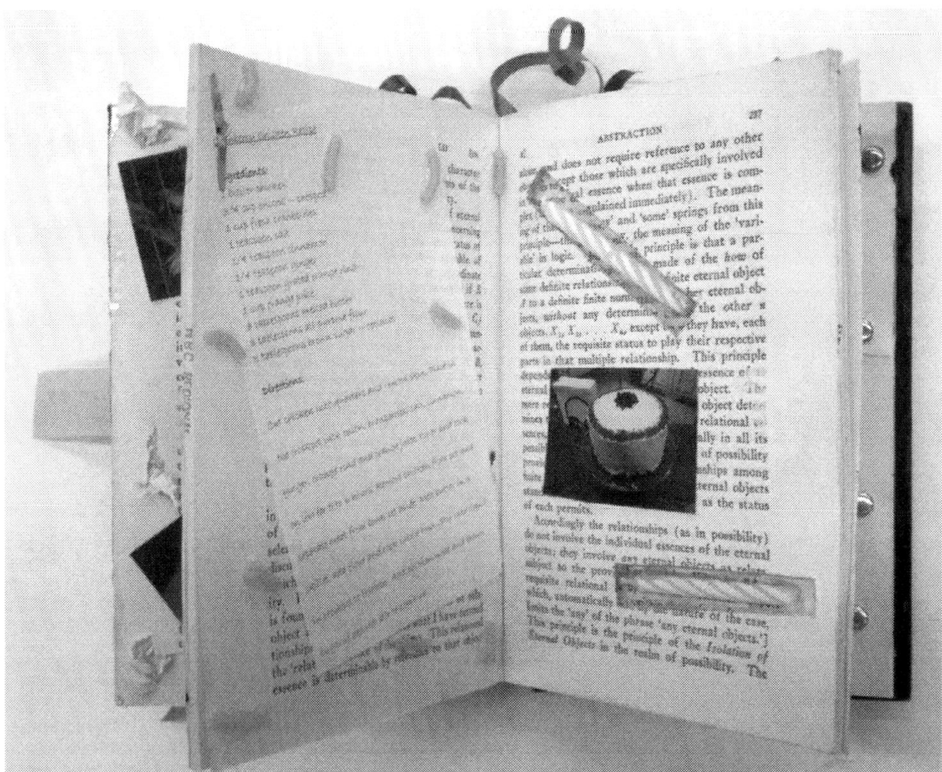

Altered book by Claire Scala

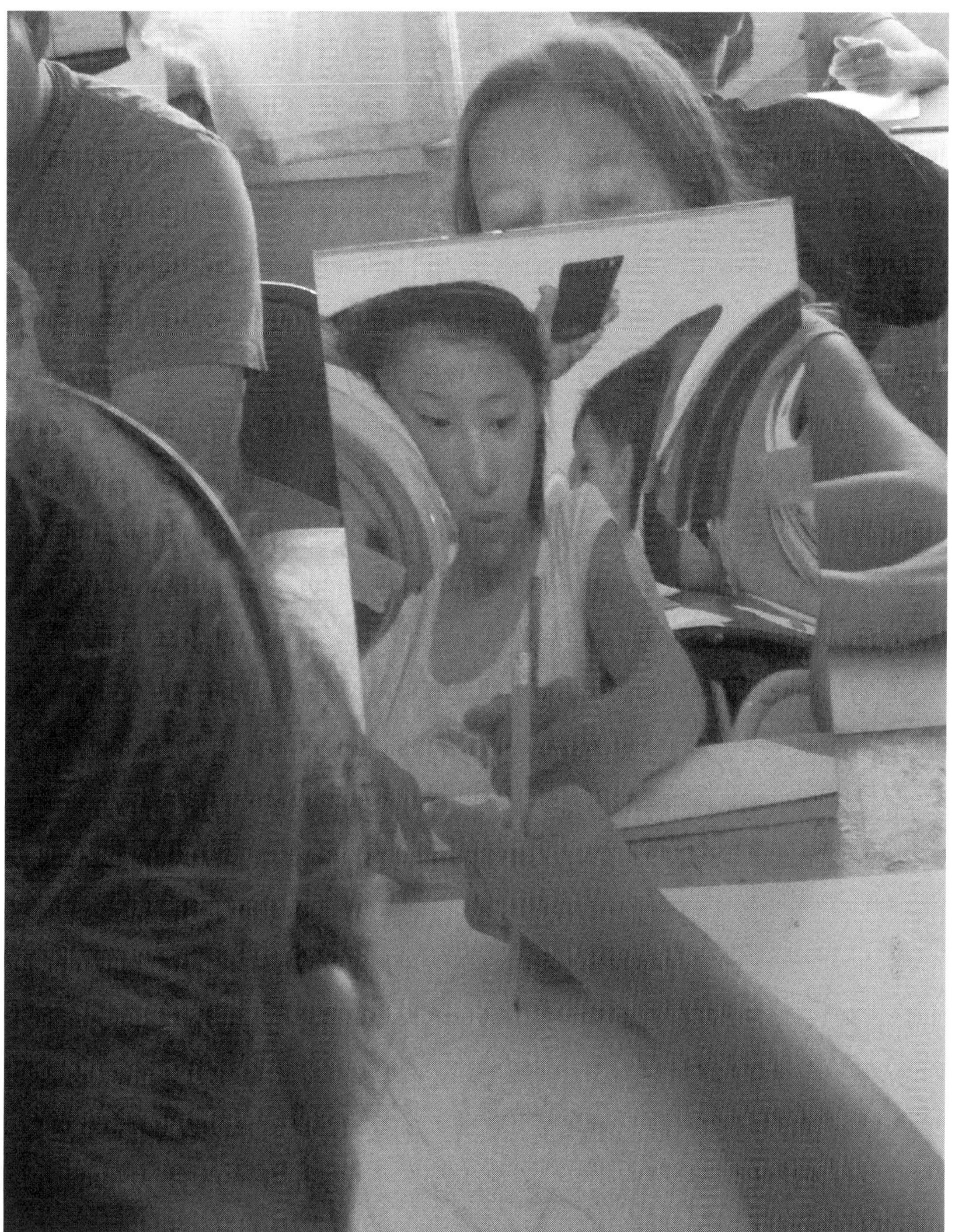

Self portraits with a warped mirror. Flexible mirrors can be twisted and warped with masking tape.

Recycled Multiples: [Problem Solving & Recycling] When available in large quantities, discarded items can be used to create modular sculptures. Cups, plastic spoons, rings, etc. They should be organized by some theme; crystals, sun sculptures, towers…

Gargoyle of Protection: [World Cultures] Students create a list of their own phobias, and incorporate a symbol that would repel that phobia into their gargoyle. (Fear of the dark?) Their gargoyle may hold a light, candle OR be created with light colors. Combine with research about gargoyles of Paris—water symbols that were to ward off fire. (Japan uses dolphin symbols)

Revelation Mask: [History/World Cultures] Students create a mask based on a symbol that reveals part of their personality people are not aware of. The Mask is created to reveal the self rather than conceal. Couple this lesson with samples of masks from other cultures or historical periods. Consider a 2-sided mask expressing inner and outer personalities.

Masterworks: [History] Students reproduce a master painting in 3-D relief with plaster of paris on canvas boards. This can be a great tie-in for an art history unit. Students could also reproduce an artwork on an unusual surface like a chair, or re-do an artwork with an element related to the student's own interest, experiences, or symbol for themselves.

Mechanisms of Unknown Purpose: [Engineering] Appeared in *School Arts Magazine*. Students bring in non-working old mechanical items and disassemble completely. (Computers, hardware, vacuum, radio, TV, etc.) They re-assemble these objects to look like some futuristic mechanism that does something mysterious. They create a name and a small story about this strange object's purpose. See example in book. Safety is an issue to consider in the destruction phase.

Viral Sculptures/Pollen Sculptures: [Science] After researching the forms of micro-organisms by either internet, library, or microscopic observation, students re-create their sample in 3-D. Often these may begin with a paper or aluminum foil base and other items added to it. String, cardboard, pipe-cleaners, wire, etc. Once the initial form is complete, students can be encouraged to embellish these forms to go from clinical to artistic. Students should note the name of their source for their form. See example in book.

Talisman: [Archeology/History] Students create a "coin" negative in clay (Oil-based clay is best) then cast plaster into the form. Students can create a coin to commemorate an event, a talisman to protect them from something, a "charm" to do some imaginary magic, or fill it with objects that represent themselves. This lesson can be coupled with a lesson in archeological discoveries of Greek or Roman coins and imperial artifacts. Students can take on the persona of Caesar & create a coin to immortalize themselves and include symbols for their own strengths and points of view.

Structure: [Engineering] In either groups or as individuals students could build a bridge with limited supplies and create a contest to see how much weight that structure could hold. (4 x 24 inch dowels, 12 inches of masking tape, and wood glue) Similarly, students could create towers with limited supplies to see whose is the tallest and can withstand a fan placed on it (Emphasizing strength and height with 4 sheets of 18 x 24 inch paper, scissors and 3 yards of tape.) Also given 50 sheets of copy paper and 3 yards of tape, students create a structure that can hold books 8 inches or more above the surface of a table. Groups can complete to see whose group holds the most textbooks.

Puppets: [History, Service Learning, World Cultures] Use non-particle carpet foam. Uniform 3-pound polyurethane sheets work well and are inexpensive, some carpet stores may even make a donation if asked. Students can create puppets of themselves, an expression of their personality, an historical figure, or specific characters similar to muppets. I find that pliers staplers are excellent for putting together puppets quickly, some glues will be helpful too but are often very smelly and toxic if air-flow is poor. Puppets can be made as historical figures, anti-bullying plays, or any subject. I like to make a performance part of the grade as well. My high school students perform for the neighboring elementary school.

Teacher Notes:

Altered Books: [Problem Solving & Recycling] *"Don't Judge a book by its cover."* Find a source for old hard cover books that are being discarded, many libraries have piles of these. Students then alter the book by painting in, cutting out, gluing in and outside the book. If you have too many books, one can be an experiment book to try out techniques, and the second for the actual graded project. Students should complete the worksheet in this book about how they are perceived by others and how they know themselves to be. Then generate symbols for these. The outside of the book should express how they are seen by others, and the inside is what they know about themselves. Encourage students to "code" their work from the worksheet about the expressive qualities of color and shape. In this way they can keep personal information private yet still express themselves.

Consumer Products: [Advertising Design, career studies] Students examine and break down the elements found on a can of soda, box of cereal, or other consumer product. They create their own consumer product that has the same elements as their samples. Label, form, logo, directions, imagery, title, subtitle, etc.

3-D Glasses: [Optics, Physics, Recycling, Environmental Sciences] By visiting most movie theatres, one may ask a manager for 3-D glasses often thrown away. Sanitize them for student use with Lysol or another cleaner. Partner with a science teacher to explore the technology of 3-D glasses and polarized plastics. They are pretty cool and do some interesting tricks. Glasses can be redesigned to become super-hero glasses by adding on sculptural elements, paint and craft supplies. They could make glasses they feel have a super power they wish they had. If you add recycled electronic items, they can look rather sci-fi high tech too. They may be painted with a theme of a particular school of art or artist. What would sunglasses look like if they were designed by Picasso, or Van Gogh? What might cubist sunglasses look like?

Wire Heads: [Self Expression/Problem Solving] Using soft annealed wire, students create a head based on their own face (Symbolically). This is then filled with objects representing things and skills that are "inside" the student. This is best coordinated with the Self Expression Worksheet early in this book to generate ideas. Inner objects can be created or actual objects brought in.

Re-Labeling: [Career Studies, Advertising Design, Recycling] Students can re-label cans or other simple consumer product. The sample soda cans were re-designed by a 4th grade class, higher grades can achieve more sophisticate results. The idea of parody can be introduced as well. Students analyze and list what elements the label must have; title, ingredients, compelling image of the product, catch phrase, etc. They use this list to check their work for completeness.

Topographical Map project by Colton Patton

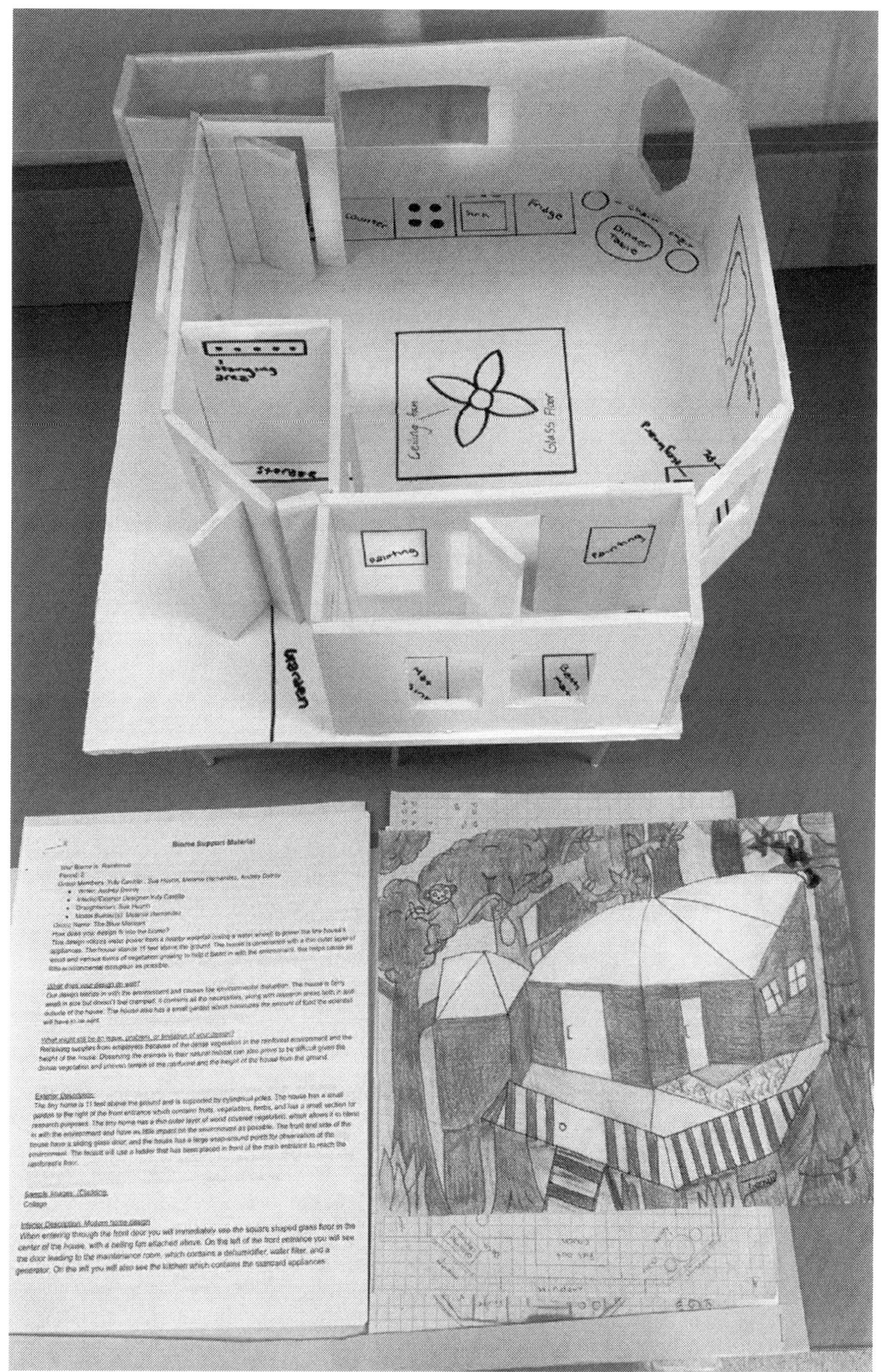

Students created "Tiny Home" outposts for a scientist to work and observe within a specific biome. This project was in coordination with an Earth Science class. www.artedguru.com/home/tiny-home-in-a-biome

Topographical Maps: [Geography] These can be created or based on real place or imaginary ones, using either plaster or paper mâché and cardboard. Start by creating a list of possible land formations and require students to incorporate a certain number of them.

Upper/Lower Coordination: [Community] Pair an upper grade with a lower grade, 3rd grade and Juniors. Have the lower grade students create drawings of the friendly monster they wish they had to protect them from something they don't like. Drawings can be colored in or left black and white. Copy and share these drawings and have upper level students. They turn the 2D images into 3D renderings with the supplies you furnish; clay, plaster, sewn fabric, paper mache, etc. Stay as true to the original as possible, but give it a professional edge, tone changes, textures, etc. Share back with lower levels and display together.

Recycled Silhouettes: [Recycling, Environment] See the work of Sue Webster. Have students use a specific light source to sculpt shadow to create an image of an object they feel is the most opposite to the recycled materials they have been given or brought. http://tinyurl.com/p459j7f (Not all the images on the website are appropriate for all levels. Please review for information)

Paper Folding: [Math, Geometry] Origami is a great way to introduce math and geometry and help students understand the relationships between shapes and how shapes can become form. Directions are broadly available on the internet as well as video tutorials to fit your own skill level from the very simple to the highly complex. http://www.origami-instructions.com/index.html is a great resource for origami models, and it's free. At the time of publication this video resource was available: http://youtu.be/bJRBiIeFe7Q
Frankenstein's Pet: [Recycling, Environment] Students bring in a pile of dolls, toys, stuffed animals, rip them apart and re-create a new monstrous creatures. Use these as part of an unusual still life project for a drawing or painting project.

Towers of Fractions: [Math, Geometry] Either by weight or volume, students create fractional units in either US measurements or metric. For example, a cube can be made that is 1 x 1 ft cubed. Given a certain fraction, students can reduce additional cubes by that fraction, be that 1/12 for reductions of an inch, or 1/2, creating a series of forms related by their fractional difference. These can then be stacked to make a fractional tower, or built in other ways to make castles, walls, or towns. The same method can be applied to creating nesting sculptures, like the famous Russian Nesting Dolls, or reductions can be done by weight with a ball of clay, and then stacked to make an "Andy Goldsworthy" style stacked stone sculpture.

Inside/Outside: [Expression] Students are given or get a box. The outside is how they are known by others, and outward stereotypes. The inside is decorated to express how they know themselves to be or things they know about themselves that others may not unless they get to know them.

Framing and Measuring: [Math, Geometry] Adding a frame or a matt to artwork incorporates a lot of measuring. Take any project from this series or another, and have students create a paper matt for it using rulers and scissors. Set standards for the matting. A rule-of-thumb among gallery owners is this; 1/4 inch overlap of the original image so that the work can be attached to the back of the frame or matt. All frame or matt sizes should be the same all the way around the artwork. Most frames are between 1 and 3 inches wide, but one must take into account that the frame must go around the perimeter. Miter cuts, or angles at the ends of the frames make for unique challenges. These are cut at 45 degrees and add unexpected length to the framing components. You may even do this lesson requiring the use of all materials without waste, forcing students to draw and measure before cutting.

Geode Crystal Creatures: [Science] There are many video tutorials on making geodes from an egg shell, food coloring, and alum. This one is particularly simple: http://youtu.be/VezcQMpIp5c After creating a geode, students can create the crystal creature that emerged from the egg. Creatures should have some color similarity to the geode, and crystalline forms should be accented.

Teacher Notes:

World Hunger Facts: [Social Studies] Students create a placemat with a fact written in the border around the matt to educate their peers. Facts should be researched and accurate. These can be found by the students or provided by the teacher. Student then create the plates, cups, silverware, and food from wire. This visually makes the ghosts of food that is not actually present. Display on a cafeteria table possibly with donation jars as centerpieces.

BackCycle: [Recycling] Find a material and research what it is made of and where it came from. Use that material to make a sculpture that relates to its original form, or from the country of its origin, or in a way that brings attention to recycling in general based on student research. Paper can be turned back into a tree, cans into what the student feel the aluminum may have been in its previous life.

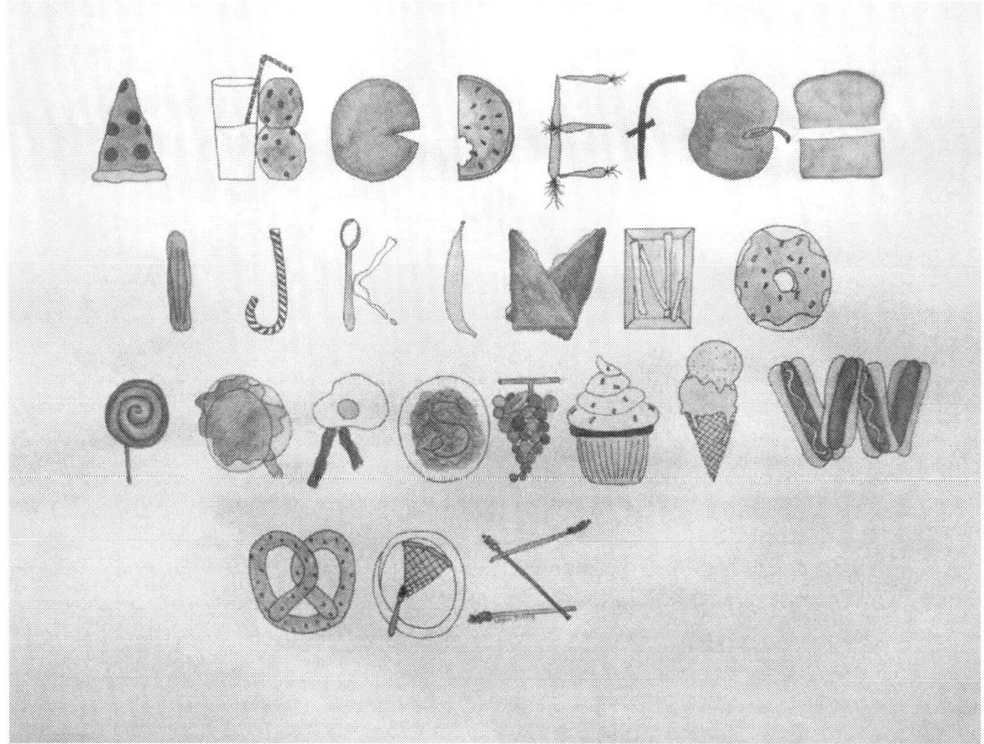
Food themed alphabet

Clay Projects:

Many sculpture based projects can be reinterpreted for clay.

Pinch Pots & Coil Pots:

A: Have students create a vessel to hold a dream, or nightmare. Do a bit of writing first to express these dreams and symbols to address the imagery or feelings. Using the page within this book about the expressive qualities of color and shape will be helpful in this.

B: Create bells by inverting the pinch pot. Create a bell to commemorate a specific achievement, or a bell to be rung upon achieving a goal you will embellish the bell with. The bell can also be a memorial to someone who has passed, or is no longer in your life, or to remember a hero who has passed.

C: Cups of friendship: Create a cup to express your feelings, or the friendship you share with another person. Often in ceremonies cups are passed between people to show the importance of relationships. An exploration of tea ceremony bowls may be apt.

D. Treasure Vessels: Create a container with a lid that holds something precious to you. It need not be a tangible item, and can even be a feeling. How will you embellish the vessel to show its importance and what it is meant to protect or keep? (Might be a good slab project as well)

E: The Anti-teapot: Create a disguised functional teapot. It must able to be filled with hot water, and pour tea but must not look like it can. Choose an object that is a symbol for yourself or something you like to do. What would a game controller look like as a teapot, or favorite pet?

F: Find a famous historical work of art you like, translate it into a functional clay vessel.

Slab:

A: Create an unconventional piggy bank to save up money for a particular goal or something you would like to buy. The container itself should be a reminder of this goal and have a slot in some place to hold the money you collect.

B: Create a miniature version of your own dream cabin get-a-way but as a bird house.

C: Create a box and embellish the inside with symbols of those things most precious to you, and symbols of your inner feelings and experiences, but embellish the outside as others see you.

D: Create a mobile chime with shapes, glazing with colors that represent the members of your family. Using the page within this book about the expressive qualities of color and shape will be helpful in this.

E. Find the image of a famous person in history that you admire or wish to emulate. Create a frame for the image of the person and decorate the frame with inscribed quotes from that person and symbols of what makes that person so important or special. This could also be done for a member of your family who is no longer in your life. (Because they have moved, or passed away)

Combined Techniques: Create a set of functional ceramic pieces that belong together; sugar bowl and creamer, salt and pepper, etc. Create them in a way that emulates a material that is not clay, like a salt and pepper shaker that looks like they are made of cut tree branches with wood end grain and bark, or a sugar bowl and creamer that look like they are made of metal with bolts and screws.

Photography

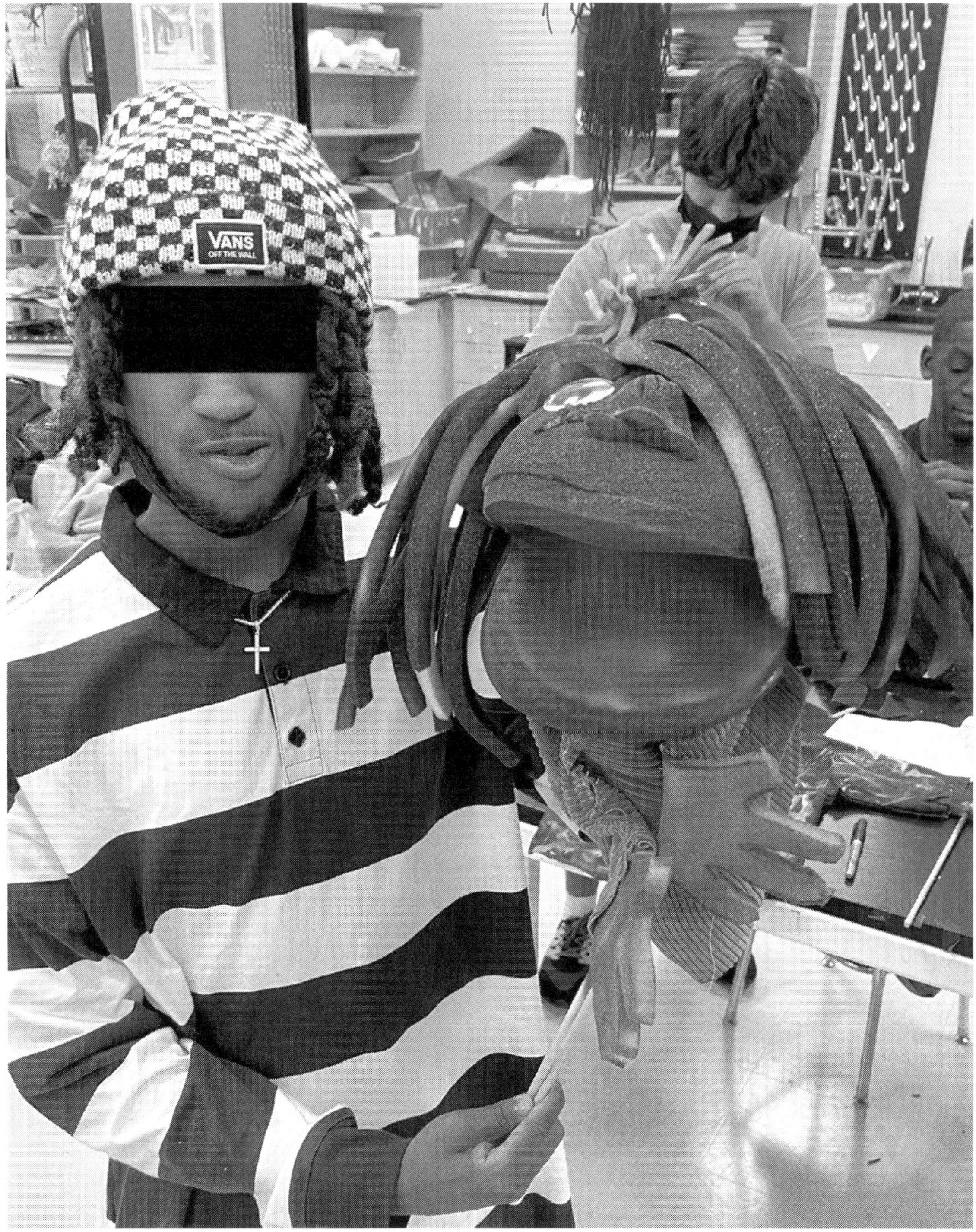

Puppetry can be a fun exploration that can be tied to a performance unit.
www.artedguru.com/home/puppet-project

Tiny Bits of Beauty: [Environment] Students find and take photos of images of easily overlooked beauty that most people miss. Enlarge or enhance the image and what makes it appealing via photo editing program.

Heritage: [World Cultures] Students research their cultural background noting animals, symbols, plants, and flags of their countries of origin, or that of their adopted family. Based on this information students create a collage of images that express their heritage or background. These can be appropriated on the internet, or created as part of the project. If their cultural flag is black, red, and yellow, take images of those hues. Translation of images need not be literal, but rooted in their cultural research.

Issue Images: [Current Events, Community, History] Students take photos of issues in their community to bring them "into the light." Research what your community is known for, its history both positive and negative. Create a single image of collage that encompasses your community from your own point of view.

Something Else: [Community, Social Studies] Students take images of something they know nothing about: Non-athletic kids taking photos of athletes, rich taking images of poor, popular kids taking on issues of bullying.

Revise Revisit: [History] Students research a given or chosen artist, finding a work of art the artist is known for and re-imagining it through contemporary photography. Warhol and creating a still life of soup cans. A van Gogh portrait of a person with heavy make-up on to emulate the artist's brush work. More samples can be found at this link: http://tinyurl.com/cer3eru

Resize: [Optics, Engineering] Students bring in their favorite miniature toy, one that they feel "speaks to who they are" as a person or a part of their persona. Create an environment for the figure to exist in but photograph it in a way that it can meld into the real world in a realistic or surrealistic way. A toy monster crushing a city, could be made with a single toy building half way crushed, in front of real buildings, and the monster propped so it appears to be within the situation. Samples can be found here: http://tinyurl.com/mcash45

Photo-bomb: [Environment] Students are given several sizes of "googly eyes" to place on object to make a visual face. Collect several for a montage of emotional faces. http://tinyurl.com/n8ma98z

Creative Cracks: [Environment] Find a cracked, broken, or worn space on a floor, wall, pavement, sidewalk, and re-imagine the space in an unusual or creative way. Can it be filled with Legos, a flower planting, books, noodles? Use this as the subject for a composed image. http://tinyurl.com/n8ma98z

Sandcastles: [Environment, Engineering] Students create paper, cardboard, or foam forms to build an elaborate castle form they wish they could live in if they were royalty. Cover this with sand, and photograph on a beach area so it looks as if it was really created on a beach. Include a play shovel and pale or other evidence that it may have been created on the beach.
Negative Spaces: [Environment] Students take images but focus on the negative spaces of their subjects. They use these negative spaces to fill with drawn or scanned artwork. They can also draw onto a print of their photograph, whiting-out the negative spaces. http://tinyurl.com/kebdjba

Teacher Notes:

All-Natural Sculptures: [Environment] After seeing the work of Andrew Goldsworthy, students create their own environmental sculpture. Students can be broken into smaller groups to make larger structures. Work should be photographed, printed, and displayed.

Selfies: [History] Students re-create historical photos into "Selfies." Students can dress up as historical figures doing what made them famous creating a "selfie." The sample link shows digitally altered images for illustration purposes, but students could create and stage images. Couple this with a writing assignment about the significance of the event or the people in the image. http://tinyurl.com/Lkf4ha5

Monuments: [History, Social Studies] Students create a memorial or monument to something they feel deserves the recognition either on a local scale or national. They create the monument, and photograph it to look like it really is within a space of the school or community. This should be accompanied with a written statement about the work and the issue.

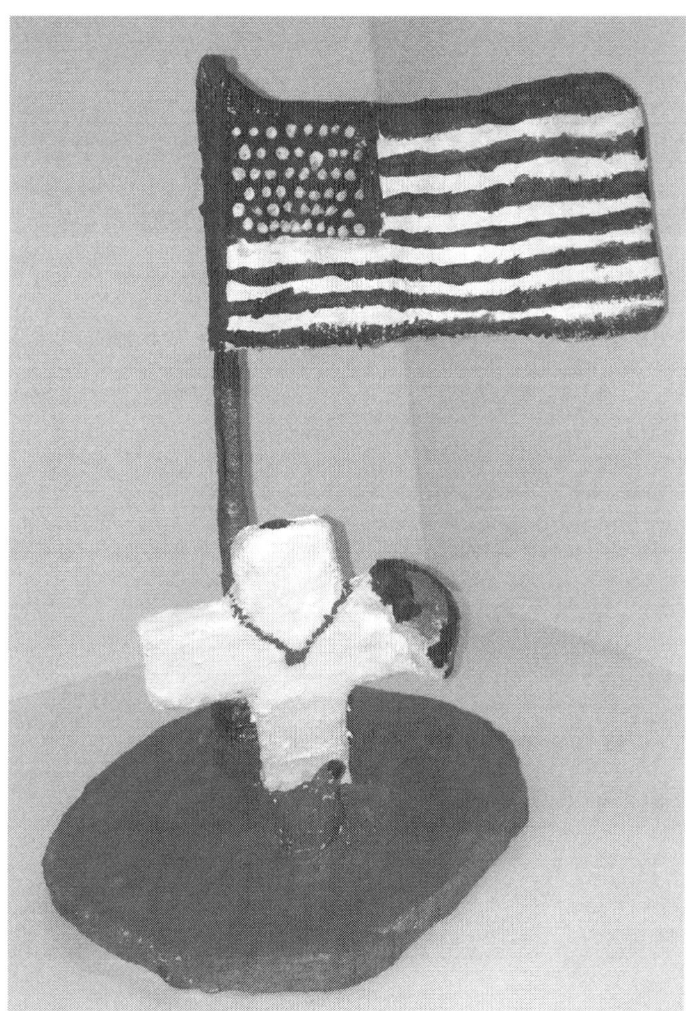

Monument Sculpture by Thomas Lindsay

Teacher Notes:

SKETCHBOOK IDEAS

Many of these may be turned into actual projects, but these sketchbook ideas are meant to be done in 1 class period or less as a way to warm up for larger projects. These are also in the student's workbooks, so if a student finishes early, they can pick something from this list to complete and stay meaningfully occupied.

Baseline Drawing 1: Draw a shoe in as much detail as you can.

Baseline drawing 2: Draw yourself in a mirror with as much detail as you can.

Baseline Drawing 3: Draw your hand in as much detail as you can.

Fill a page with scribbles, and then look at them and reveal what can be seen in them. This is similar to looking at clouds and spotting objects in them, but here you color them in.

Rip a random small piece of paper from a magazine and draw it. Enlarge it to fill the page.

Draw the view through a window.

Write your name 30 times, in different sizes and directions, overlapping often to divide the page into many shapes. Color in using colors that express your mood today using the expressive colors and shapes worksheet.

Draw a tree from your imagination then draw a tree from observation. Which looks better to you? Why?

Trace your hand in an interesting position and turn it into an animal. DO NOT MAKE A TURKEY.

Find a common small object and enlarge it to fill your paper.

Draw yourself in a mirror but DO NOT look at the paper while you do it.

Draw a friend or family member with one continuous line. Do not lift the pencil until it is complete.

Find a tree and draw what is seen between the branches without drawing the tree itself.

Find a face in a magazine or photograph, turn it up-side-down and draw it up-side-down too.

Fill a page with shapes, get into every corner, but DO NOT lift your pencil until you are done. Color in using colors that express your personality using the expressive colors and shapes worksheet.

Draw some clouds from observation.

Draw your hand holding a CD. Draw as much of yourself in the mirror as you can see even if it is just a fragment.

Trace a leaf, trace the shadow it makes. Color in as realistically as you can like trompe l'oeil.

Trace your hand in an interesting position; fill it with patterns and color that express what you like to do with your hands.

Draw what you have in your pockets right now.

Draw a shoe, position the laces in such a way as to create a hidden face in your show. Draw it realistically but be sure to capture the idea of a face as well.

Take 2 unrelated objects and create a hybrid image of this new object. (Like scissors and a bird)

Spy on someone and draw them without them knowing.

Draw your meal or utensils.

Half fill a clear glass with water. Place 1 or 2 objects inside that are both in and out of the liquid (like a spoon or chopstick), draw it.

Take a common object that would relate to yourself, then repeat that object to make an animal that you also feel expresses your personality. Feel free to abstract and stretch the objects to make your animal.

Get a new pencil, do a drawing of something around you by holding the very end where the eraser is.

Write your name and a short statement in block letters, maybe a poem or memory, BUT do it with your eyes closed. Color in after you are done.

Using only color and shape, try to do a drawing that represents LOVE without using a heart.

Do a drawing of the feeling of WAR with colors and shapes and NO objects. Try other words.

Do a hybrid drawing of 2 unrelated animals as a new animal (lion & fish maybe). Be sure to have examples of both in front of you if possible.

Set an object in a box. Draw the object in the box; include the inside of the box in your drawing.

Draw an outline of a simple object.

- Draw the object again without lifting your pencil.
- Draw the object again without looking at your hand while you draw. Try to do it with a mostly continuous line.
- Draw the object's outline and shade with crosshatching lines.
- Draw the object again and use scribble lines to create shadow.
- Draw the object again only using dots for color and shadow.

Take a pattered fabric or shirt, drape it over a chair and draw it showing the pattern changes as the fabric folds and drapes.

Draw an object from observation above. Color the light side with warm colors (yellow through red) and the shaded side with cool colors like purple, blue, and green.

Put together a group of similarly colored objects. Set them up on a contrasting or opposite color for a still life drawing.

Draw a flag that would represent your family. Try to be symbolic. Use the worksheet in this book on the expressive qualities of shapes and colors.

Draw something from an unusual point of view.

Draw your hand drawing your hand in a funny way. (M.C. Escher did something like this)

Find a small simple, common object. Draw it large and turn it into an architectural design.

Draw your head realistically or as a cartoon. Add a large hole or opening to it and have objects escaping from that hole that tell a story about what goes on in your mind.

Trace an object about the size of this page, onto a page. Turn it into a very different object by how you finish the drawing. A pair of scissors may become a bird. You may add onto the object as you wish, try not to erase much of the original outline.

Cover half of your face with an object, and then create a self portrait.

Draw an original super hero with a power you wish you had.

Draw a stabbed object. (Like a piece of fruit with a pencil stabbed into it) Make the drawing with exaggerated sense of emotion.

Draw someone talking. Fill the background with their words in a creative way. This could be a historical figure or someone around you today.

Draw something flying that would not normally be able to fly.

Write an expressive word in large fat bubble-letters. Fill in the letters with images that relate the meaning of the word.

Draw an animal based on a photograph of it, BUT only draw it with letters found in its name. It is okay to abstract the letters to make them fit. Use the colors of the animal to finish it.

Design an item of clothing, color and texture it.

Draw the kind of house you would like to live in.

Draw your hand pointed away from you toward an object, draw both your hand and the object. Overlap a bit if you can to add realism and a hint of perspective.

Use candles, burn sticks and draw a still life with home-made charcoal.

Draw a wall with windows, and details of adjacent items like bookshelves, chairs, etc. Then draw an unexpected environment through the window.

Draw yours or a friend's face, divide it into 4 parts, and color each section with symbols for 4 things that are important to that person.

Trace your hand and draw what might be inside if you were an awesome robot.

Paste down half a face from a magazine. Choose an attractive model. Finish the other half of the face as if they were an alien.

If you could design your very own cell phone, what would it look like?

Draw a container, and on the back draw something unexpected that would be inside the container. Hold the page up to the light to see an x-ray view of both.

Design a piece of jewelry and use a symbol from your own cultural background in it.

Draw a piece of foil with a few wrinkles in it.

Place a coin under a page, rub a pencil over the page to create an embossed image. Then draw your hand holding the coin.

Draw a design you think would make a cool tattoo for you. Remember that tattoos are often symbolic of thing important to the person wearing it.

Draw the *thing* that lives under a child's bed.

Draw someone's ear from about 6 inches away from them. Be so close you can see every detail.

Using a flashlight, draw an object and its shades and highlights, but light it from an unusual point of view. (Like a face with the light below the chin, or still life lit from below.

Crumple a page, flatten it lightly so the creases are still obvious, then draw the page.

Draw a CD cover for your favorite song.

Draw your home as a castle but include details that are there right now.

Crumple this page, lightly flatten it, and trace the wrinkles making what you can imagine into the creases. This is similar to finding objects in clouds. As you stare, object will become apparent.

Draw something dry as if it was wet.

Have a friend lay down on the floor. Draw their portrait while sitting above their head so their face is up-side-down. Your drawing will be up-side-down as well.

How would you re-design your hand to be better than it is? If you were into basketball, how might it be different? Consider your hobbies and activities.

What might a flower look like on an alien planet?

Design a new cologne bottle for either a great scent, or something very bad.

Willy Wonka remade an environment out of candy, what would you draw an environment out of?

Create a new label for your favorite beverage.

Pick a playing card and do a design based on that card that no linger looks like a playing card. Use repetition and pattern if it helps.

Create a cover for a ridiculous comic book.

Draw something in the room no one notices.

Lay on the floor and look up. Draw part of the room with this unusual perspective.

Put your leg up on the table and draw your leg, shoe and all, in perspective.

When you cross your eyes, you see double. Draw something around you as if you had double vision. Find a creative way to handle overlapped areas.

Do a portrait of a friend, but re-imagining their hair in a way that shows off their personality.

Draw the trophy you wish you could win.

Draw the first thing you would buy if you won the lottery.

Draw your hand holding your favorite possession.

Draw what it looks like sitting in the front of your car, and put something unexpected in the rear-view mirror.

Draw something pretty next to something ugly.

Draw a piece of popcorn to fill this page.

Draw something floating in a magical way.

Hold a tube of paper up to your eye and draw your point of view. (If you have glasses, maybe you can tape a small tube to them.)

Stand on something tall and draw your view looking down.

While lying on the floor, draw what you see from that perspective as if you were a bug.

Draw an object that makes noise. Draw what you imagine that noise might look like if it could be seen.

Sit in the back of a bus or car and draw your point of view. Feel free to change the scene through the window or make it realistic.

Draw something lit by a candle.

Draw two objects side by side that should never be put together.

Draw two objects side by side that represent opposite themes: War and peace, good and evil, love and hate…

Make a drawing that expresses a lie either literally, figuratively, or symbolically.

Draw an object as if it were in-side-out.

Draw the surface of a coin with a water droplet on it. If you have a magnifying glass, use it.

Draw a soft object with a steel skin with screws, rivets, and bolts.

Draw a cute animal as if it were Frankenstein's pet.

Draw an animal you consider unappealing, as cute.

Draw an object from observation but re-arrange its parts in an unexpected way.

Draw an advertisement for a product you would not like but make it seem appealing.

Draw two objects side by side but change their scale. For example, you might have a giant ant next to a tiny teacup.

Crumple a picture from a magazine and draw it as you see it.

Design a new kind of chair.

Do a line drawing of your shoe, and color it in the way you think would look interesting.

Life is often full of choices. Draw a portrait of yourself, divide the face in half, and show two potential life choices you will need to make as an adult in the design. (You as a teacher or you as a hairdresser) Use symbols and colors in the portrait to show the possible directions your life might take.

Take a common object and draw it as if it was a skeleton. What would the skeleton of a pear look like?

Design a monument for a common object, like a monument to a thumbtack.

Draw a face card from a deck of cards making you the queen, king, jack, or joker.

Draw what you see reflected in a bowl or plate of water. It will reflect better if the bowl is a dark color.

Draw your home or backyard from an aerial perspective. (From above)

Draw a mysterious doorway.

Draw how you would symbolize the 4 seasons.

Design a metal of honor commemorating your greatest achievement in your life so far. If you do not have one you can think of, consider an accomplishment you hope to achieve in the future.

Re-imagine the wrapper for your favorite candy bar. Create a new design for it.

Do a drawing of an object you possess or have nearby, but make it look like its melting.

Draw an object that is reflective. Add a portion of your face into that reflection. (Cell phone, CD, compact, glass of water, spoon, Christmas ball…)

Try to draw an object from 3 points of view but as one object. This is how cubist painters like Picasso and Braque would work.

Find an object and only draw the things around it, leaving the paper white where the object is. We call this negative space drawing.

Scatter a few objects on your table; only draw the parts that overlap.

Draw a landscape with a house, car, or man-made object in it. Give the man-made object natural textures like leaves and grass, and give the natural elements mechanical textures found in the object.

Do a portrait from very careful observation but rearrange the parts of the face.

Create a holiday or birthday card cover in the style of a famous artist.

Do a drawing from observation so lightly that only a person close to the paper can see it.

Draw someone eating, and illustrate behind them, expressive colors, textures, and shapes that you feel would describe the flavor.

Draw the back of someone's head. Try to capture hair without resorting to scribbles.

Draw an eating utensil morphing into something else.

Draw your bedroom as if it was inside a container like a teapot, jar, cardboard box…

Ask the closest person to you pick an object in the area, and then draw it.

Place a few objects on a white piece of paper, only draw the shadows.

Draw what you imagine the inside of your stomach looks like after the last meal you ate.

Imagine you ARE your favorite animal. Do a drawing you think that animal would draw if it could or from its point of view.

Draw a fun pattern for a necktie or bow.

Draw an amazing sand castle on the beach.

Write your initials very large and turn it into a drawing of animals, objects, or other subject.

Draw a new and unique sea creature.

Draw a new and unique dinosaur.

Draw a how-to label or poster for something you know how to do. If it is too complicated, illustrate just 1 to 4 steps of the process.

Draw a simple cartoon that illustrates the last time you were embarrassed.

Draw something with wings that normally would not have them.

Do a drawing of a person combined with an animal. The Egyptians did this a lot.

Create an advertisement for yourself as if you were a product in a store.

Create your initials in a very ornate and decorative way, like old illuminated manuscripts.

Remove your socks and shoes and draw your foot.
How would you redesign a common road sign? Yield, Stop, No Running, Poison...

Draw yourself as if you were 100 years old.

Quick Project Assessments *(next page)*

As you look at your work, use the rubric below to grade your own work on the next page. You can add a plus or minus if you feel the need. Your teacher will also grade your work and their grade is the one that is recorded. If your grade and the teacher's grade are different, you can have a conversation about the differences so on the next project you can better meet the expectations.

Neatness:

A. Is not folded, ripped, cracked, smudged, wrinkled, or messy look. Pristine project condition.
B. Mostly not folded, ripped, cracked, smudged, wrinkled, or messy looking.
C. Mild folds, or rips, or cracks, or wrinkles, or smudges.
D. Having more than one issue with folds, or rips, or cracks, or wrinkles, or smudges.
F. Substantial folds, rips, cracks, wrinkles, or smudges.

Completeness:

A. No empty areas. Completely colored, consistent handling, having more than the required elements.
B. Mostly no empty areas. Mostly colored, consistent handling and most required elements.
C. Some empty areas. Having some areas of consistent handling and some required elements.
D. Several empty areas. Having significant areas of inconsistent handling, and few required elements.
F. Work does not approach complete and has significant deficits in material handling and elements.

Originality:

A. Not copied, 100% student generated idea, genuine uniqueness or novel point of view.
B. Not copied, student concept generated with some assistance, unique point of view.
C. Not Fully Original, possibly a collaborative concept, references used to generate similar ideas.
D. Substantial copied or derivative ideas with some unique aspects, considerable assistance required.
F. Not original; copied or fully derivative

Following Directions:

A. Going step by step in process, not skipping steps, novel use of materials and unique handling.
B. Going step by step, mostly not skipping steps, mostly taking ones time to use materials as instructed.
C. Following most directions with some missed steps or shortcuts, some deficits in material handling.
D. Missing many steps and/or significant shortcuts. Several deficits evident in material handling.
F. Steps and/or directions generally ignored more deficits than not in material handling.

Meeting Project Goals:

A. Having surpassed all required elements, exceptional project depth of concepts and expression
B. Meeting required project elements. Strong use of expression and project concepts.
C. Meeting most project required elements. Good use of expression and/or concepts.
D. Meeting few project required elements. Few examples of expression and/or concepts in final work.
F. Includes nearly no required elements, expression, and/or concepts.

Teacher Only Resource: https://youtu.be/yhieQG6rC04

Student Workbook has 2 pages like this

Assessment: Graded by both the teacher and the student. Only the teacher's grade counts, but if there is a large difference between the assessments, they can be discussed.

Project Title ________________________________ Date Complete ______________
Short Description ____

Assess a grade of "A, B, C, D or F." You may add + or – if you feel the need.

Student Assessment Below		**Teacher Assessment Below.**		
Neatness	_____	Neatness	_____	
Completeness	_____	Completeness	_____	
Originality	_____	Originality	_____	
Following Directions	_____	Following Directions	_____	_______
Meeting Project Goals	_____	Meeting Project Goals	_____	Recorded Grade

---

Project Title ________________________________ Date Complete ______________

Short Description ____

Assess a grade of "A, B, C, D or F." You may add + or – if you feel the need.

Student Assessment Below		**Teacher Assessment Below.**		
Neatness	_____	Neatness	_____	
Completeness	_____	Completeness	_____	
Originality	_____	Originality	_____	
Following Directions	_____	Following Directions	_____	_______
Meeting Project Goals	_____	Meeting Project Goals	_____	Recorded Grade

---

Project Title ________________________________ Date Complete ______________

Short Description ____

Assess a grade of "A, B, C, D or F." You may add + or – if you feel the need.

Student Assessment Below		**Teacher Assessment Below.**		
Neatness	_____	Neatness	_____	
Completeness	_____	Completeness	_____	
Originality	_____	Originality	_____	
Following Directions	_____	Following Directions	_____	_______
Meeting Project Goals	_____	Meeting Project Goals	_____	Recorded Grade

---

Project Title ________________________________ Date Complete ______________

Short Description ____

Assess a grade of "A, B, C, D or F." You may add + or – if you feel the need.

Student Assessment Below		**Teacher Assessment Below.**		
Neatness	_____	Neatness	_____	
Completeness	_____	Completeness	_____	
Originality	_____	Originality	_____	
Following Directions	_____	Following Directions	_____	_______
Meeting Project Goals	_____	Meeting Project Goals	_____	Recorded Grade

Assignment: ______________________

Universal Art Project Rubric

	Criteria				Points
	100% / 20pts Exceeds Expectations	90% / 18pts Meets Expectations	80% / 16pts Approaches Expt.	70% - 65% / 14pts Missed Expt.	0/F
Project Requirements	*I exceeded expectations by:*	Expected use & combination of art elements & principles. Work included all requirements.	Acceptable use of art elements & principles but lacked depth in exploring requirements.	Lacks evidence of thoughtful use of elements & principles with a design that looks unplanned, rushed, &/or incomplete.	___
Material Care, & Completeness	*I exceeded expectations by:*	Overall, the project is clean & without major defects like Folds/Rips. All areas have been considered & finished to meet expectations.	Minor folds or stray marks may be present but the work is acceptable. Some portions of the work could have benefited by more attention to detail.	Work includes obvious deficits like folds, rips, &/or stray marks. Little effort went into creating the work & using information demonstrated.	___
Time & Management	*I exceeded expectations by:*	Student was mostly independently motivated with a few social distractions. Work was mostly self-driven.	Student was somewhat distracted from their work **OR** finished early without using the extra time to push the depth or quality.	Often reminded to stay on task. Social/digital interactions impeded work. Lack of focus had a strong impact on project work.	___
Detail, Complexity, & Craftsmanship	*I exceeded expectations by:*	Materials & techniques were explored & met project expectations. Many visual challenges were attempted.	Media or technique was not fully explored. Visual challenges were minimal.	Media & techniques show little evidence of exploration. Visual challenges were avoided.	___
Original, Personal, & Unique **(Always credit your inspirations)**	100% original & highly personal because:	Generally personal, & unique but inspired by:	Topically personalized and based on:	Topical and highly derivative of:	Copied
Comments:				**Grade**	___

Students write & <u>underline</u>/highlight, teacher circles & makes notes/comments.

Assignment: ______________________

Universal Art Project Rubric

	Criteria				Points
	100% / 20pts Exceeds Expectations	90% / 18pts Meets Expectations	80% / 16pts Approaches Expt.	70% - 65% / 14pts Missed Expt.	0/F
Project Requirements	*I exceeded expectations by:*	Expected use & combination of art elements & principles. Work included all requirements.	Acceptable use of art elements & principles but lacked depth in exploring requirements.	Lacks evidence of thoughtful use of elements & principles with a design that looks unplanned, rushed, &/or incomplete.	___
Material Care, & Completeness	*I exceeded expectations by:*	Overall, the project is clean & without major defects like Folds/Rips. All areas have been considered & finished to meet expectations.	Minor folds or stray marks may be present but the work is acceptable. Some portions of the work could have benefited by more attention to detail.	Work includes obvious deficits like folds, rips, &/or stray marks. Little effort went into creating the work & using information demonstrated.	___
Time & Management	*I exceeded expectations by:*	Student was mostly independently motivated with a few social distractions. Work was mostly self-driven.	Student was somewhat distracted from their work **OR** finished early without using the extra time to push the depth or quality.	Often reminded to stay on task. Social/digital interactions impeded work. Lack of focus had a strong impact on project work.	___
Detail, Complexity, & Craftsmanship	*I exceeded expectations by:*	Materials & techniques were explored & met project expectations. Many visual challenges were attempted.	Media or technique was not fully explored. Visual challenges were minimal.	Media & techniques show little evidence of exploration. Visual challenges were avoided.	___
Original, Personal, & Unique **(Always credit your inspirations)**	100% original & highly personal because:	Generally personal, & unique but inspired by:	Topically personalized and based on:	Topical and highly derivative of:	Copied
Comments:				**Grade**	___

Students write & <u>underline</u>/highlight, teacher circles & makes notes/comments.

Pre-Project Writing 1

(Not in student edition)

Describe the idea of the project: (*Write about it as if you were talking over the phone*)

____

____

____

____

____

How might I personalize the project so it is unique to me?

____

____

____

____

____

What part of the project do you feel you'll do well with and why?

____

____

____

____

____

What part of the project do you think will be most challenging and why?

____

____

____

____

____

What resources can you use if you get "stuck" along the way? Who or what can help?

____

____

____

____

Sketch a preliminary idea on the back of this paper.

Pre-Project Writing 2

(Not in student edition)

What are the requirements for this project? *(Materials, subject, elements, ideas, ...)*

What materials will you be using?

What techniques will you be using or learning about?

What "rules" or procedures must be followed as you work? Any safety concerns?

(Storage, work-area set-up, clean-up, tool use...)

What connections can you make in this project to work you have done in the past?

(History, previous projects, material handling, expression...)

Sketch a preliminary idea on the back of this paper.

Ordering Supplies

These are the supplies I order for 1 year of both sculpture and a general art classes.

Budget: I consider the number of students I see on an average day, and divide that by the supply budget to get an idea of what I am working with, and in some ways, judge how well the school supports art education. I run a fairly vigorous 2D and 3D program without clay, so my $40 per student serves me well. If I had to add clay, then something else would have to be set aside. I know many teachers operate with far less, so I have a blog post with ideas to help. That is found on this webpage: https://www.artedguru.com/home/art-upplies-on-a-zero-budget

The following are supplies I order on a regular basis for 150 students seen daily for 1 year.

6 reams of 11 x 17 inch drawing paper
3 reams of 18 x 24 inch paper
3 reams of 11 x 17 watercolor paper
1 ream 18 x 24 watercolor paper
100 16 x 20 inch canvas board
20 doz. Sharpie fine point
20 Doz. Sharpie ultra fine point
6 set Sharpie color pack of 24 (2 varieties)
2 gallon acrylic gloss medium
4 cans clear acrylic spray paint
50 doz. Sargent #2 Pencils
3 pencil sharpeners
1 gross erasers
1 six pen set Sakura
24 rulers 12 inch
6 box latex gloves
1 drying rack
2 packages of "Flawboard" 100 pack
12 packs of ¼ inch dowels
6 cases of plaster craft
12 rolls of 5 lb stovepipe wire, 20 gauge
6 rolls of 5 lb stovepipe wire, 16 gauge
12 long nose pliers with cutter
24 jumbo eye needles, 5 inch
4 rolls of aluminum sheet metal (NOT foil)
2 packs of pipe cleaners, multi-color x1000

If there is enough money I would also order metallic acrylic paints & some spray paint. Order some tools like hammers, hacksaws, blades, hand-held drill & 1 set drill bits.

6 pint of blockout white acrylic paint
6 pint of acrylic paint Mars Black, ***and all colors*** you may need. Go heavy on primaries.
24 sets of water color pencils 24 colors
3 tubes "Kiss off" or other stain remover
2 bulk set of 144 brushes rounds & flats
4 rolls craft paper 1000 ft. x 36 in. 2 white/2 brown
20 sheets of 3/16 foamcore
20 sheets ½ in foamcore
12 X-Acto knives
5 packs of X-Acto blades of 100
12 bottles rubber cement
12 bottles 7.5 oz. Elmer's Glue
6 bottles carpenter's glue
527 glue (good for plastics & metal)
4 box glue stick
4 hot glue guns
400 hot glue refills
60 rolls assorted masking tape
10 bags of casting plaster 25 lbs
1 container of Vaseline 12 oz. (inexpensive release agent for plaster)
2 Rube-r-mold kits
10 packs of 1 oz. cups/ 250 cups (lids?)
5 packs 3.25 oz. cups and lids / 250 cups
5 packs 3.25 oz. cups and lids / 250 cups
10 rolls of aluminum foil 12 in. x 200 ft.
10 bottles speedball ink

Often what is purchased in one year can be used the next year.
Here is a list of some supplies I recommend:

- Craft Sticks / Popsicle Sticks
- Junk Brushes (cheap house-painting brushes)
- Plastic plates
- Buckets, sponges, rags
- Rubber buckets for plaster work
- Disposable aprons
- Yarns and string
- Nylon kite-type string
- Acrylic rods for construction
- Scrap or copy paper
- Construction paper
- Storage bins for wet work
- Wood scraps in bulk
- Nails, pins and fastening devices
- Mirrors, small and or large
- Miniature Mannequins
- Clips, tacks, binders & folders
- Glitter and minimal craft-like items
- Speedball pen tips
- Clay if you have access to a kiln
- Bulk markers, pencils, crayons, oil pastels
- Modeling clay (non-hardening)
- Drawing boards
- Rubbing alcohol
- Paint thinner (odorless)

Some Art/Math Answers
NOT in student edition

1. $166.664
5. Multiply length by width
6. 70, 70, 166
7. 16 x 21
8. 74 inches or 6 ft 2 in.
9. 216 in^2
10. The ends of rulers are often worn
14. NO: Your materials cost you money.
18. Black has more pigment that is more dense.
19. Different for every brand, you must calculate and use a scale. Weigh white, add black in small amounts till gray is correct, re-weigh and calculate.

We are always looking to make improvements, if you spot errors in this edition you wish to make us aware of, or have a lesson you think should be included, please email the author directly. For significant help, at our digression, we offer a free copy of the book as a thank you. LOVSART@gmail.com or contact us via our website: www.FirehousePublications.com

10 Rules of an Art Museum Visit

Art Museums are special places, housing, saving, and conserving art for the world to see. It is not like visiting a regular public space, and there are some rules to observe.

If you get lost or need assistance please call this number ________________________

- Don't make cell phone calls or text while in museum exhibitions
    - It's rude and disruptive to the museum experience for others.
- Don't eat in the museum exhibitions.
    - Museums often have cafeterias where you can eat a snack.
- Your phone should be set on vibrate or a very low sound.
    - We may need to find you if you're late.
- NEVER touch works of art. Even finger prints can damage art.
- Photography is sometimes forbidden. Ask a guard if you are not sure.
    - **DON'T assume it's ok if others do it.**
- NEVER use flash photography, Turn off your camera flash.
    - Light can damage the colors of some work
- Whisper or remain silent. Please don't cause distractions.
- Many people see art museums like churches for art--very special places, so be respectful.
- Take your time to SEE the art and think about what the artist was trying to say.
- DO pay attention to the time and our schedule:

NOTES:

Museum Assignment Name ______________________________ Period ____

While in the museum, you have an assignment that will be collected and graded. Please find and sketch 3 artworks as described below. Please write a response for each in full sentences.

1. Sketch an artwork you see in the museum that you have seen in class or somewhere else. If you find no work that you recall from outside the museum, choose a work that really impressed you.	2. Sketch a work that surprised you in some way.
3. Sketch a work you feel you liked but could be improved upon. How would you improve it?	4. Find & sketch the oldest work in the museum you can that is attributed to a single artist. Title ________________________ Artist ___________________ Date ___________

QUIZ ANSWERS

Art Elements

1. Line is the simplest art element and is needed to draw anything.

2. Shape is the art element that is 2 dimensional. The basic ones are these three:

3. Triangle

4. Circle

5. Square (any order for these 3)

6. Texture can sometimes be made by repeating an art element.

7. Light helps things look 3D in a drawing or a painting.

8. Color is reflected light. When we use a prism, we can see all of its components in white light.

9. Form is a shape in 3-D or a 3 dimensional art element.

10. Draw and shade ALL the basic 3 dimensional "shapes" below.

(Sphere, Cone, Cylinder, Cube)

Art Principles

1. Unity creates a sense of "sameness" to hold everything together visually.

2. Variety keeps things from getting too boring by adding visual differences.

3. Contrast offers opposites to make the differences more obvious, even shocking sometimes.

4. Movement gives a sense of motion, either real or by design.

5. Balance makes a work feel settled, or complete on both the right and left in most cases. This principle is done in 2 ways, they are:

6. Symmetrical

7. Asymmetrical (Any order for these two)

8. Pattern is a repeated design. It can be natural or mechanical.

9. Emphasis makes one thing or area stand out more than the rest.

10. Illustrate & label one principle below.

Individualized Results.

Art Class First Survey: (Student Workbook Page 5)

First and last name printed ____ Period _____-______ Grade _____

Define Art: ____

____

How many years of art class have you had before this class? _____________

What do you feel your artistic ability is right now? 1 to 10 ________ (1 = NO ability at all, 10 = I'm pretty good at art.)

What do you hope we do in art before the end of the year? ____

____

What would you like to get better at before the end of the year? ______________________________________

____

Name some art elements (Line is one...) ____

____

Name some art principles (Balance is one...) ____

____

What is your favorite thing to draw, doodle, or make? ____

Even if it's not art related, what's your favorite hobby or "non-school activity" ____________________________

____

What are 4 words you would use to describe yourself ________________________, ______________________,

____________________________, ____________________________, bonus word? ____________________

Sometimes schedules change at the beginning of the year, or you got a class you didn't expect and think you might want to change your schedule. Check off the statement you feel is true for you.

[__] I chose this class. [__] I did not choose this class so I might switch. [__] I will be switching out, 100%!

On the next page, draw the person sitting next to you. Their name is ___________________________

End of Class Survey: (At the end of the Student Workbook)

1. What was your favorite project of the year/semester and why?

____

____

2. What was your least favorite project of the year/semester and why?

____

____

3. Did you feel the teacher was able to allow you enough freedom to express your own "artistic voice?" Please give an example of your experience here.

____

____

4. What was something you learned that you feel you will remember most?

____

____

5. What is the most positive thing you can say about having art class?

____

____

6. What advice would you give your teacher to consider for next year?

____

____

7. Anything else you might like to say or share?

____

____

____

Draw the person sitting next to you on the next page and compare this to your first drawing.

Who did you draw? ______________________

Compare this drawing with the one you did in the beginning of this workbook

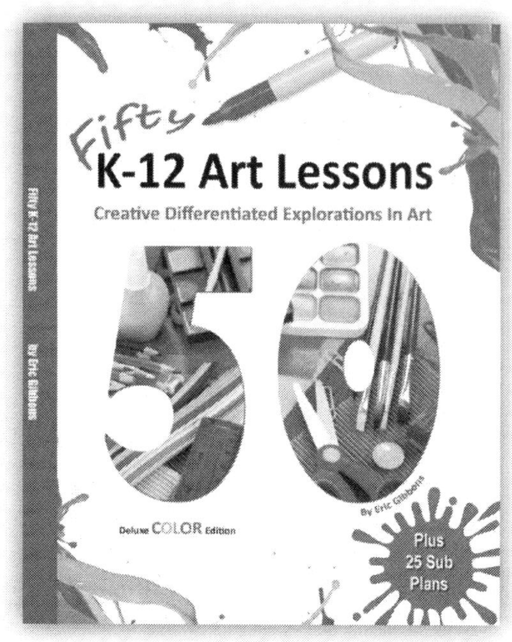

More resources at www.FirehousePublications.com

Made in United States
Orlando, FL
29 June 2024

48409679R00122